P9-CCM-916

CHESS FOR BEGINNERS

A Comprehensive and Simple Guide to the Best Strategy Game, its Openings, Strategies, Tactics, and Much More. Discover Why You Cannot Play Chess Unless You Know the Gambits

ROBERT QUEEN

Table of Contents

© **Copyright 2020 - All rights reserved.**

The content contained within this book may not be reproduced, duplicated or transmitted without direct written permission from the author or the publisher.
Under no circumstances will any blame or legal responsibility be held against the publisher, or author, for any damages, reparation, or monetary loss due to the information contained within this book. Either directly or indirectly.

Legal Notice:

This book is copyright protected. This book is only for personal use. You cannot amend, distribute, sell, use, quote or paraphrase any part, or the content within this book, without the consent of the author or publisher.

Disclaimer Notice:

Please note the information contained within this document is for educational and entertainment purposes only. All effort has been executed to present accurate, up to date, and reliable, complete information. No warranties of any kind are declared or implied. Readers acknowledge that the author is not engaging in the rendering of legal, financial, medical or professional advice. The content within this book has been derived from various sources. Please consult a licensed professional before attempting any techniques outlined in this book. By reading this document, the reader agrees that under no circumstances is the author responsible for any losses, direct or indirect, which are incurred as a result of the use of information contained within this document, including, but not limited to, — errors, omissions, or inaccuracies.

Introduction

Chess is a fascinating game for many reasons. Many people want to play it, but only a few finally end up learning how to do it. The reason for this is not hard to guess: chess is simple to learn, but it takes patience to perfect the art of playing it. Even when you have perfected the art, you still need to improve your skills daily. So, when many people just look at all they have to go through to learn the game, they simply decide to give up. Nevertheless, chess remains an interesting game that anyone should learn to play and actually play for various reasons.

Often, when some people want to learn how to play chess, they don't usually know where to seek guidance. Sometimes, the available materials are disjointed and not organized in a logical way to offer a hierarchical flow of information. That's the main reason why I have written this simple guide to teach anyone, regardless of age, gender, or prior knowledge how to play chess. The guide is written in simple language, devoid of any form of unnecessary jargon. This is to make the learning process easy for you.

Even though this guide is for beginners, it is also recommended for people who already know how to play chess but want to improve their skills or learn new moves. As I said earlier, the guide is simple to follow and understand – it is devoid of superfluous information. I have also tried as much as possible to make lesser use of texts to explain concepts and moves. Rather, I have used proper diagrams to make the explanation of concepts and moves easier for you to understand.

Chess already appears like a daunting task and a difficult game to learn – so, I don't intend to complicate things further. Each chapter will lead directly to the next, with the level of difficulty only varying slightly.

With that being said, it's time for us to get to business without further ado. Happy learning.

Chapter 1:   Brief History of Chess

In the earliest forms of chess, it was known as the game of four divisions, representing the military and its divisions. India received the game from the Persians, where it was part of a noble's education. As the rules developed, players would yell "King" or "The King Is Helpless!" two phrases that over time would turn into what we know today as check and checkmate.

Islam continued the spread of chess, with the pieces keeping the names originally assigned to them from the Persians. As time went on, chess spread throughout the world. By the 9th century, the game had reached Western Europe and Russia. Traders brought special chess pieces throughout their travels.

In fact, the first chess pieces documented in Western Europe came from Muslim traders. Variations popped up in various cultures, from Buddhism to China. In the Far East, the game was played on the intersections of the lines versus in the squares themselves.

Once chess had spread to Europe, it developed and took shape, becoming very similar to what we know as chess today. In the modern history of chess, rule and competitive play have become part of the game. Chess teams in high schools and colleges play for the honor and accolades of their school, even if there aren't as many individuals to cheer for them that understand the game.

Like any other game or sport, charismatic players have increased their popularity. But let's take a step back to India for a look at how chess was played in the 6th century.

In India, the earliest form of chess was called Chaturanga. This game had two features that survived into all other variations of chess, which was the not the same pieces having not the same abilities and that declaring the winner depended on the fate of one piece. Today, that piece is the king.

Chess was designed to be played on an 8x8 squared board. This board was originally used for backgammon type race games and adapted to the game of chess. The name Chaturanga literally means four limbs or parts. These four parts, for the purpose of the game, comprised the parts of a military force in that time period, namely the elephants, horsemen, chariots, and then the foot soldiers.

It is this tie to the military that had chess dubbed a game of military strategy, as those who played it most frequently were either commanders or kings, both of which would be in charge of soldiers. Early forms of chess may have been played using dice, which decided the piece that would be moved.

There is an unproven theory that chess itself started as a dice game, but gambling and dice were removed over religious objections, namely Hinduism, which is one of the primary religions in India. Still, that military background continued, and chess was used as a tool for strategy, gambling, mathematics, and even some astronomy.

The chess pieces themselves were made of ivory, a material prevalent in India at the time. In some variants, wins could be made by virtue of a stalemate, where the king was the only piece left to your opponent.

Early chess moves were assigned by the piece. As a result, each piece could only be used in certain ways, but these moves varied from Persia, India, and Southwest Asia.

The king has remained the dominant piece. The queen can move one square diagonally at a time.

With the bishop, the moves it could perform depending on the location where the game was being played. In Persia, the bishop could move two squares diagonally, but could also jump over any piece in between. The Indian version said the bishop could move two squares sideways or front and back but could also jump over a piece in between. Southeast Asia limited the bishop to only one square diagonally or one square forward. The knight and rook have the same abilities we see in modern chess, which we will cover.

The pawn could move one square forward and capture one square diagonally forward but must be promoted by the queen.

One of the earliest games was recorded from the 10th century between a historian and his pupil in Baghdad. In the 11th century, a raja visiting from India used a chessboard to explain past battles.

Chess pieces started out as elaborate pieces of art in themselves, depicting animals and other ornate pieces. In Islam, however, the pieces were assigned names and abstract shapes because Islam forbids the depiction of humans or animals in their art.

In China, the game was altered to where the pieces were placed on the intersections of lines and not within the squares themselves. The whole point was still the same as with the chess from Persia and India, which is to disable the king, rendering it helpless.

Sometime around 1200, the rules of chess began to change in southern Europe, with these changes forming the base of chess as we know it today. Pawns gained the ability to advance two squares on their first move. Additionally, bishops and queens were given their modern moves. The stalemate rules were finalized in the early part of the 19th century. This form of chess became known as Western chess or international chess, distinguishing it from other versions, including historical ones.

As the game of chess evolved, theories began about the best ways to win. Clergymen developed various opening elements and they analyzed simple endgames. In the 18th century, the center of chess life moved to France. There were two French masters, one a musician named Francois-Andre Danican who discovered how important pawns were for strategy; another was Louis-Charles Mahe de La Bourdonnais, who won a series of chess matches with Alexander McDonnell, an Irish master. Coffee houses became centers of chess activities, especially in big European cities. These coffee house matches were the beginning of chess organization, such as chess clubs, books, and journals. There were matches between cities even, thus beginning the birth of the sport of chess.

Birth of Organized Chess

Howard Staunton, an English chess player, organized one of the first modern tournaments back in 1851. London was abuzz when the winner, an unknown German named Adolf Anderssen. He was hailed for his energetic attacking style, typical of the time. Over time, the nature of chess became as much a source of debate as the game itself. The idea of anticipating attacks and then preparing for them became a scientific approach that attempted to create and exploit the weaknesses of your opponent.

Wilhelm Steinitz revolutionized the game by breaking down a position to its components. He created defenses and strategies that depended more on the other pieces, instead of simply striking quickly with the queen. In 1886, he was regarded as the first official World Chess Champion. He lost his title to a German mathematician Emanuel Lasker, who retained his title for 27 years and is widely hailed as one of the longest world champions in history.

Moving into the 20th century, the number of tournaments and annual matches grew. For example, in 1914, Tsar Nicholas II of Russia awarded the title of Grandmaster of Chess to five men, although it was disputed. The World Chess Federation was founded in Paris around 1924. The Women's World Chess Championship was founded in 1927. Throughout the world wars, chess continued to grow. New theories, such as the hyper modernists who believed in controlling the center of the board with distant people, inviting the opponents' pawns into the center, and then attacking them.

After WWII, an era of Soviet dominance in the chess world occurred. American Bobby Fischer was the only champion that interrupted the Soviet dominance, until the end of the Soviet system of government. A system of matches was developed during this period that allowed for the strongest players to be seeded into tournaments. From these tournaments, individuals would go to the chess version of the playoffs, gradually reducing their number until one was left. That one would play the reigning Champion for the title. If they won, the original Champion would be able to challenge them again in one year. Everything moved on a three-year cycle, so a champion was crowned every third year.

These tournaments continue to this day, with the last one being held in 2013. But what was the effect of chess on the culture?

Chess was part of the culture of nobles during the Middle-Ages and the Renaissance. It was a teaching tool of war strategy and even morality. The chess pieces were used as metaphors for the various classes and the duties of individuals came from the rules of the game or the properties of the pieces themselves.

In modern culture, chess became a means of self-improvement. Benjamin Franklin said it helped us to gain foresight, circumspection, and caution, skills which are important in real life. This train of thought has continued to hold true to some degree, as the game of chess is taught in schools and tournaments have been created specifically to reach out to children.

Within the arts, chess itself has been depicted as a key to the greater story. Films such as Ingmar Bergman's The Seventh Seal use chess as a key to the struggle of the two protagonists.

So now that we have looked at some of the history of the game, let's learn about how to play it!

World's Famous Chess Players

- Bobby Fischer

- Magnus Carlsen

- Garry Kasparov

- Joshua Waitzkin

- Paul Murphy

Chapter 2:   How to Play Chess

Rules and Chess Notation

The object of the game is to threaten the opponent's King with a move that will lead to an inevitable capture or checkmate.

The player holding the White pieces makes the first move and the players make alternating moves afterward. Each player is required to make a move at every turn. In major tournaments, a computerized draw is made to determine who will be holding the White pieces.

If the King is in check, the only legal move a defending player can make is to get the King out of check. The player may move the

King out of the threatened square, capture the attacking piece, or use another piece to block the attacking piece.

The game ends when the King is captured, a draw is declared by an arbiter, or a player resigns.

En Passant

En passant is a pawn maneuver that allows an opponent to capture a pawn "in passing". It can only happen under the following conditions:

- The capturing pawn is on the fifth rank.

- The opposing pawn moves two squares from its first position instead of only one square to avoid capture by the enemy pawn on the adjacent column.

Instead of replacing the captured piece in its position as in all other instances of capture, the capturing pawn takes the position that the opponent's pawn would have taken had it chosen to advance one square away from its first position.

The move to capture the passing pawn must be made immediately after the opponent's turn. If it happens to be the only possible legal move, the en passant capture must be made.

Castling

Castling is a maneuver involving the King and one of the rooks. It is the only chess move that allows a player to move two pieces in one turn, the only other move where both pieces can mimic the knight's ability to jump over other pieces, and the only move where a King is allowed to go two squares away from its original position.

Castling may be done on the King's side or the Queen's side. If done on the King's side, the King moves 2 squares to the right while the Rook moves 2 squares to the left. If carried out on the Queen's side, the King moves two squares to the left as the Rook simultaneously moves three squares to the right.

Castling is allowed only if all of the following requirements are met:

- The King and the Rook involved are in their original position and have never moved prior to castling.

- There are no pieces on the squares between the Rook and the King.

- The King must not be in check at the time of castling. In other words, castling cannot be used as a move to evade a check. If the player intends to castle, the threat must first be eliminated by either capturing the attacking piece or blocking it with another piece.

- The King must not end up in a square that will place it in check after castling.

Castling is an important strategy in the opening as it allows the player to move the King to a safer position while simultaneously moving the rook to a more advantageous attacking position in the center. Kingside castling is generally more preferred because it requires less movement to accomplish, places the King in a relatively safer position closer to the board's edge, and allows the King to support all three pawns on the castled side.

If it's not possible to castle as in cases where either the King or the rook were forced to move before, they can castle, a player may prefer to keep the King safe by taking additional moves to accomplish what is called Artificial Castling.

Moving the Pieces

Only one hand should be used to move the pieces. Once the piece is released on a square, the player will not be able to retract the move unless it is illegal. Castling is done by moving the King first with one hand and moving the Rook using the same hand.

Once a Pawn has been released on the eighth row with the intention of promoting it, the player is obliged to promote the

Pawn by replacing it with a new piece. The promotion is not final until a new piece is placed on the square.

Touch-Move Rule

While the rule is not strictly followed in informal games, the touch-move rule is in effect during serious games. Under the rule, provided that the piece can be moved legally, the player must move a piece once it is touched. If the player touches an opponent's piece, the piece should be captured if there is a possible legal move to do so. If there are no available legal moves to capture or move a piece, no penalty is imposed on the player. A player who wishes to touch a piece to adjust its position on the square must first inform the opponent of his intention to adjust the piece before doing so. A player may only touch a piece for whatever purpose when it is his or her turn to move.

The touch-move rule likewise applies during castling. A player who touches the Rook and the King at the same time must castle using the same rook provided the move is legal. If the King moves two squares towards the direction of a Rook, the Rook must be moved to complete the castling. If the castling is illegal, the King must be returned to its original place. The player must then move the King if there is a possible legal move.

Check and Stalemate

Each player strives to capture the opponent's King to win the game. When the King is under threat of capture by an opponent's piece, it is said to be 'in check'. The 'check' is generally announced in informal games, but this is not required during competitions.

Once under 'check', the player must immediately address the threat. Here are possible moves to get out of check:

- Move the King to a safe square.

- Block the path of the attacking piece by placing another piece in between. Take note that this option is not possible if the attacker is a Knight or a Pawn. A piece used to block the threatening piece may simultaneously place the enemy King under check.

- Capture the attacking piece if another piece is in a position to do so. The King itself may make the capture if the action will not place it under check. Take note that it is illegal to move the King in a square where it will be placed immediately under threat of capture.

If it becomes impossible to get the King out of check, it is 'checkmated' and the game ends. The player with the 'checkmated' King loses the game.

Draws

A draw is a tied game in which neither player wins the game. A draw may be automatic or claimed. A draw is invoked using the following rules:

- stalemate

- 50-move rule

- threefold repetition

- checkmate impossibility

- mutual agreement

A stalemate may occur if the player taking turn is not in check but lacks the option to make a legal move. This situation results in an automatic draw.

The game may also end in a draw when both players have made 50 moves each without a capture or a pawn's movement. The draw may be claimed by either player.

If the position is repeated thrice by the same player, he or she can claim a draw. The claim should be made before the third move is made. Otherwise, the player will lose the opportunity to claim a draw. A player who decides not to invoke the three-fold repetition rule may claim a draw afterward in the game if a similar opportunity presents itself. In 2014, FIDE added a rule that allowed an automatic draw in cases where the positions are repeated by both players for five consecutive turns.

The game may also end in a draw if neither player lacks the capability to checkmate the other player based on the remaining chess pieces. For instance, it will be impossible for the game to result in a checkmate if the remaining pieces are king versus king, king versus king and knight, king versus king and bishop, and both kings with a bishop each on the same square color. A King may still win when left with a Pawn if the Pawn can be promoted.

Any player can offer a draw at any point in the game, but a draw will only be declared if both players agree.

Resigning

A player may opt to resign anytime during the game. The decision to resign is usually made if the player foresees an inevitable loss either by a checkmate or time expiration. A player may either verbally state his wish to resign or tip the King on its side.

Time Control

The length of a chess game is controlled with a timer or a digital game clock. FIDE, the World Chess Federation, sets a limit of 90 minutes for the initial forty moves and an additional thirty minutes for the remainder of the match with an increment of thirty seconds per move counting from the first move. This is for standard games, however, and game time may always be adjusted for special games. Informal chess games are usually played without the benefit of a game clock.

Recording Chess Games

The moves in a chess game can be recorded and described using different methods. The present standard is the Algebraic Notation, but you may also come across old chess books using Descriptive Notation. Recording is required in official chess competitions for use in case of disputes or in situations where the application of chess rules require information on the type and number of moves made. Knowing how to record and read chess games is important if you seriously want to improve your playing skills.

By writing your own games, you will be able to recheck your moves and have the game replayed. Knowledge of notation will also allow you to study and learn from great games played by champion players.

The Algebraic Notation

Each square on the chessboard is assigned a unique code. The columns (files) of squares starting from the leftmost column on the queen's side going to the right are labelled a-h while the rows (ranks) starting from the White's side are numbered 1-8. The position of a piece is identified by the coordinate letter-number pair. For instance, the White Queen's starting position is on d1 – the square located on the fourth file and first rank. The Black King's staring position is on e8 – the square on the fifth file and eighth rank.

You will use the following standard symbols in reading or recording chess games:

K	King
Q	Queen
R	Rook
N	Knight
B	Bishop
x	Captures
+	Check
++ or #	Checkmate
ep	En passant
O-O	Castling on the King's side
O-O-O	Castling on the Queen's side

Chapter 3:   The Fundamentals of Chess

How is Chess Played?

Before one can start in the game of chess, they should be familiar with its objective, the pieces used to play the game, and which moves can be done by the player.

Chess is a two-player game in which the win condition is to threaten the opposing player's King so that it won't be able to avoid getting captured (also called a checkmate). Players can eliminate the pieces of their opponents by moving their own pieces so that they can get closer to their goal.

The "game field" is a board with 8 rows and 8 columns of boxes with alternating colors that are similar to a checkered flag. Each column is designated with a letter (A to H) from left to right, while the rows are assigned with numbers (1 to 8) starting from the bottom. Rows are called *ranks* while columns are called files.

The image in the following page shows what a chessboard looks like and the starting position of all the pieces. It also shows the imaginary numbers and letters in the board that shows the positioning of each piece.

The pieces are either white or black. Players take turns making one move per turn, and the game starts with white always making the first move.

All About Chess Pieces

The game of chess is like a battlefield wherein the soldiers of each general (or player) are the pieces.

Each player is provided with 16 pieces that should be placed in their starting positions accordingly. These pieces, depending on what they are, can only be moved in a certain way, which are as follows:

- Pawn - Each player has 8 of these. Pawns can only move one square forward at a time except for their first move, as they can move 2 squares forward from the starting position. Pawns have a different way of capturing an opponent's pieces, as they can only eliminate opposing pieces diagonally forward one square, either to the left or to the right. Their starting positions are on the 2nd rank for white and the 7th rank for black.

- Rook – This looks like a tower and can move horizontally or vertically for any number of squares as long as those squares are not blocked. It can capture opposing pieces that are within the area of their movement range. Each player has 2 rooks. Their starting positions are the corners of the game board.

- Knight – This piece looks like a horse (and sometimes called as such). It can move in an L-like fashion; that is, from its initial position, the player should move it two squares either horizontally or vertically, and then move it one square to the left or right. So long as the player can draw that imaginary L when this piece moves, it is legal. The place where it should land is the square that it can capture. Because of this quality of the knight, it can "jump over" other pieces as long as its landing spot is unobstructed. Players have 2 knights, and those are placed beside the rooks.

- Bishop – This can move any number of squares diagonally depending on the color of the square where it is placed (determined by the starting position), and can capture opposing pieces in its movement range. Both players are given 2 bishops and they start next to the knight.

- Queen – The queen can move to any unobstructed square after moving diagonally, vertically, or horizontally. Players only have 1 queen at the start of the game and are placed on the square beside the bishop that corresponds to the piece's color (White's queen occupies the light-colored square next to the bishop while Black's queen occupies the dark-colored square).

- King – The king can move one square in any direction except when castling. Each player has one King, and it is placed beside the Queen.

Point Values of Each Piece

A player can have an idea of the advantage that they have over their opponent based on their point differences.

Each piece in the game is assigned with a numerical value, and a player gets points depending on the pieces that they have captured during the game.

The point values are as follows:

- Pawn = 1 point

- Bishop and Knight = 3 points

- Rook = 5 points

- Queen = 9 points

The king has no assigned value since it cannot be captured. These point values are directly proportional to their contribution to the game. For example, since the queen has more liberty when it comes to its moves, it has a higher value compared to other pieces that have some form of limitations.

To apply this concept, let's say that you are able to capture your opponent's bishop while he is able to capture your knight. Since both pieces have the value of 3 points, the game is not yet in any player's favor. However, if you able to capture the opponent's rook but he can only get a bishop, it can be seen that you now have an advantage when looking at the points of each captured piece.

Think of these point values as the power level of each side. As the game goes on, the goal is to significantly decrease the power level of your opponent and ensure that yours is higher. This also implies that in order to analyze the game carefully, they simply need to look at how many points are remaining for them and their opponent.

Playing the Game

After getting to know how all your pieces work and what their strong and weak points are, you need to arrange them on the board in order to start your game. First, you need to make sure that the light-colored square is located at the bottom right corner of the players. You don't want to play on the wrong side of the board. After which, set up your pieces in the following manner:

1. Make sure you have 16 pieces complete, all having the same color.

2. Position all of your eight pawns on the second row in front of you.

3. Next, position each rook on both corners on your side of the chessboard.

4. Place one Knight beside each rook and then place a bishop next to it.

5. Then, position the Queen in one of the two remaining spaces. If your piece is light-colored, place it on the light-colored square. If it is dark-colored, then place it on the dark-colored square as well.

6. Lastly, place the King on the last space remaining. Try to check if the opposite side has a similar arrangement as yours with the Kings and Queens opposite to each other.

30

When everything on your board is in place, you are now ready to start your game. In playing the game chess, one must also remember the following things:

1. The player with the light-colored pieces makes the first move. They can pick any piece that is allowed for movement; pawns and horses. The players take turns in playing and it is not allowed to make two successive movements at any point of the game.

2. Depending on the strategy you want to use, try to position your pieces to their most useful posts. You want your pieces to be in safe and good squares in order to avoid having more pieces captured than that of the opponent.

3. Each move you make should only be done using only one hand. Also, remember that you cannot move two pieces at a time except in the special move called castling.

4. In this game, there is what we call a touch-move rule, which states that you should move the piece you already touched unless if it places the King in a check. This is a basic rule in chess that is why it applies to every game, except if the players agreed beforehand not to adhere to it. In addition to this, if you touch an opponent's piece, it must then be captured if possible. If it's not, then the game continues as if it had not been touched.

5. However, if you want to adjust or align your pieces properly, you can do so without committing a touch-move by saying in advance that you are going to move a piece. Notify your opponent first so that you will not encounter any conflicts during the game.

6. The ultimate end goal of the game is to capture the King. All your strategies and movements must lead towards this goal. To emphasize it again, the King must be protected at all times because once you lose it before your opponent does, then you lose your game.

7. When moving your other pieces, try to keep track of whether each move will put your King to risk. Also, look at your opponent's every move. Do not become too relaxed at any point of the game so that you can detect threats and possible attacks by the opponent.

8. During the whole duration of the game, try as much as possible to think a step or two in advance. If you move once piece, try to think about what happens after. Does it expose the other pieces or does it go into a position where you can play offense or defense? It is important to plot your movements with tact, proper timing, and strategy in order to increase your chances of winning the game. Take time in preparing your every movement to avoid mistakes and miscalculations.

9. The game must be conducted in a manner with utmost respect for the opponent. A player must not do things that will annoy or distract the opponent. It is important to maintain an honest and fair game.

The main goal of the game is to capture the opponent's King. But through the course of the game, it is necessary to capture other pieces in order to gain advantage over the opposing side. A piece captures an opponent by moving and replacing the square it occupies. The piece is then removed from the chessboard after having been captured.

Chapter 4:   How the Pieces Move

Do you know of a situation that gets all your mental faculties alert while the rest of you is calm and collected? Well, the game of chess is one such situation. Chess is simply the game to keep you young, confident, and razor-sharp.

It is a 2-player game where each player tries to outmaneuver the other until the other player loses his or her king. King...? Yes, king. In ancient days when monarchies were the order of the day, if your king was captured, you did not have much of a country to talk about. The power was in enemy hands and you had no choice but to surrender. That is pretty much how empires were created. In chess, however, the king is part of the playing pieces. And like those ancient kings, this one is well guarded.

What Playing Pieces Are There in Chess?

Well, each player has 16 pieces. And to play good chess, you need to know the rules governing the movement of each piece. The idea is to keep as many of your pieces safe as you capture as many of your opponent's. And at the end of the day, your big target will be your opponent's king as you pull out all the stops to protect your own.

Here are the chess pieces:

King

King reigns supreme and without the king you have no game. Whenever your king is under direct threat, it is said to be in check and you may hear your opponent exclaim, 'check.' This draws your attention to the looming danger and your following move should be geared towards protecting your king. You can bring in another piece to block the danger posed to your king or you can relocate your king to safety. The king is allowed to move in any direction as long as it takes just a single step.

In case there is no move you can make within the rules of play to protect your king, then your king finds itself in the position referred to as checkmate. Checkmate means that your king is totally exposed and has no escape route – the king must be captured.

As for the level of activity, you do not need to move your king a lot especially in the early stages of the game and even the middle game. However, it comes in very handy during the endgame. Each of the two players has each one king.

It is important that you don't get too excited about capturing your opponent's pieces that you forget to put the King's safety first. Here below is a situation where your opponent's piece is under attack from the King and yet the King cannot follow through and capture it.

	A	B	C	D	E	F	G	H
8	Rook	Knight	Bishop	Queen	King	Bishop		
7	Pawn	Pawn		Pawn		Pawn		Pawn
6		Bishop						
5								
4								
3					Rook	King		
2	Pawn	Pawn	Pawn			Pawn	Pawn	Pawn
1	Rook	Knight	Bishop	Queen		Bishop	Knight	Rook

Ignore all the other chess pieces and focus on the colored ones on the chessboard above. Do you notice that the black Rook is under direct attack from the White King? Yet the King won't capture it because doing that would put the King under direct attack from Bishop at b6. So, even if it means losing an opportunity to capture a piece, the King can never put himself at risk of being captured. For the same reason too, you'll never find the two rival kings placed side by side.

Queen

The queen has the best ammunition to protect the king – that, in the form of unlimited moves. You can move your queen however you wish and for whatever distance you wish – in a straight line horizontally; vertically; and even diagonally. That flexibility of movement makes the queen the most powerful piece in the game. Each player has a single queen which is symbolically placed after the king. There is, however, a tact that you can use to create a second queen as you will see. Just so you know, there was a time the queen was referred to as the minister – just for being devoted to the king.

Rook

This piece used to go by the term castle once, and still, some people called it tower; rector; or even marquess. However, even when calling a rook, a castle is seen as archaic, the term castling is still in use. It simply means moving your king to a spot you consider safe.

Each player has two rooks, each placed at the end of the first row of the chessboard. The rook pieces used to symbolize chariots and chariots were well-armored transport vessels in which the king would ride. The castle was also considered a secure place; so, for this piece, it is all about ensuring the king is in a safe place.

When it starts let the rook at the same place as the knight and bishop continue to the empty squares made by pawns. Afterward in the game is when you will realize the real value of your rooks. Rooks provide great support to your pawns during the end game.

And how does a rook move? Well, forwards, backward, and also sideways – simply put, horizontally and vertically. And for distance, the rook can move any number of squares in the chosen direction, as long as the squares it is passing are not occupied by any pieces. That makes it quite versatile even without room to move diagonally. Just remember, the rook doesn't hop or jump.

Knight

This piece, which comes in twos for each player, is very dangerous to the opponent. That is why you need to take it where the real action is – in the middle of the chessboard. As you will soon see, the knight can easily clear any of eight squares for you as long as you know how to position it. This book will teach you how to utilize such pieces to their fullest and not waste their potential.

Physically, this piece looks like a horse's head with its neck. As the game begins, each of your knights is positioned one square from the edge on your first row – actually after to the rook, on the inside.

And as for its moves, the knight moves in an L-shape, made up of a 2-square move followed by a 1-square turn. You can also move your knight one square in one direction, followed by two squares in a different direction to complete the L-shape; and the results will be the same. The knight, just like a real horse, can jump over things; this one over other chess pieces, till it reaches its target.

You also need to appreciate how handy it is like a playing piece considering it doesn't often have to wait for other pieces to give way so it can land where it wants. This is particularly important during the opening of the chess game when for other pieces to move, a way has to be created by pawns. You will soon notice how suited a knight is a fork execution.

And that's a fork in chess?

Well, it's that move where the piece you have played ends up threatening two of your opponent's chess pieces concurrently. If you hear the term, double attack in the game of chess, this is it in other words. As for the chess piece that is threatening to do damage, it's referred to as the forking piece, while those pieces under attack are described as being forked.

In case your opponent manages to protect one of those forked pieces in the subsequent move, then you are left with one forked piece. BUT – in case that piece which your opponent uses to protect the forked piece is stronger than the forking piece, consider that piece which was under attack still forked. In short, your opponent's piece is still forked if the value of your forking piece is lower than that of the piece your opponent brought out as a protective measure.

Here are some beautiful forking examples:

	A	B	C	D	E	F	G	H
8	Rook	Knight	Bishop			Bishop	Knight	Rook
7	Pawn	Pawn	Pawn	Pawn		Pawn	Pawn	Pawn
6						King		
5							Queen	
4					Knight			
3								
2	Pawn	Pawn	Pawn	Pawn	Pawn	Pawn	Pawn	Pawn
1	Rook		Bishop	Queen	King	Bishop	Knight	Rook

Without worrying much about how the players got there in the chessboard above, can you see that any move the white knight makes will capture either the King or the Queen? Remember the knight moves in an L shape – 2:1 or 1:2 squares. In fact, the King has been checked as it is now.

The move NxQg5 is inevitable. Reason...? The black player can only save one of the two pieces in the following move. Obviously, the piece to save must be the King because to do otherwise would be suicidal – capture the King and the game is over.

	A	B	C	D	E	F	G	H
8	Rook	Knight	Bishop			Bishop	Knight	Rook
7	Pawn	Pawn	Pawn			Pawn	Pawn	Pawn
6				Queen		King		
5					Pawn			
4								
3								
2	Pawn	Pawn	Pawn	Pawn		Pawn	Pawn	Pawn
1	Rook	Knight	Bishop	Queen	King	Bishop	Knight	Rook

Recalling that pawns move only a single square forward and capture by moving one square diagonally, can you see that in the chessboard above the pawn has the option of capturing either the Queen or the King? That's real forking.

Obviously, Black will make the King run for safety one way or the other, but the Queen cannot escape capture here.

	A	B	C	D	E	F	G	H
8		Rook	Bishop	Queen		Bishop	Knight	Rook
7	Pawn	Pawn		Pawn	King	Pawn	Pawn	Pawn
6								
5					Queen			
4								
3								
2	Pawn	Pawn	Pawn	Pawn	Pawn	Pawn	Pawn	Pawn
1	Rook	Knight	Bishop	Queen	King	Bishop	Knight	Rook

Which two pieces are forked in the above chessboard? Obviously, the King, who is for all practical purposes under check; and the Rook, which is directly in the Queen's path with no other piece in between.

As usual, Black saves the King by moving him hastily to safety while the Rook is, inevitably, captured by the Queen.

Bishop

This is another piece on the chessboard that comes in twos for each player. Each of your bishops will sit three spaces from the edge of your chessboard on your first row – one between your king and knight and the other between your queen and knight. If you observe well, you will notice that while one of your bishops is on a light-colored square, the other is on a dark-colored one. Consequently, the one on light square proceeds to move along the light shaded squares while the one on dark square proceeds along the dark shaded squares. For that reason, during the game, there is the tendency to refer to each as either light-squared or dark-squared accordingly. Alternatively, you may hear them referred to as either king's or queen's bishop depending on where one was placed at the start of the game.

The bishop moves diagonally only and displaces any enemy pieces it finds in its way. It is not limited in the number of squares it can move. However, it does not go over other pieces to reach the enemy. In that regard, it is like all the other pieces with the exception of the knight.

So, you better cling to your bishops when you see vast open spaces on the chessboard. But the minute you realize that spaces are cluttered somewhat, you may consider exchanging your bishop for a knight. Remember the knight has the flexibility of movement – including jumping over other pieces. Can you see why chess is not a routine game? It keeps your mind alert to see how conditions are changing, so that you can adjust accordingly.

Pawns

Each chess player starts off with eight pawns. The pawn is often seen as the weakest piece of all, probably because you can only take it one square forward – straight ahead or diagonally: not horizontally. Of course, the only exception in distance is when the pawn is seated in its original position where you have leeway to move it two squares forward at a go. And a pawn cannot move backward.

Chapter 5:   Strategies for Beginners

Section 1 – Checkmate

The purpose of both strategies is to enhance one's chances of success in any endeavor. In chess, success is determined by victory, and victory is determined by checkmate.

Checkmate occurs when a player's king is under threat of capture from one or more enemy pieces and cannot make a legal move to a safe square. When this happens, the player whose king is trapped loses, and their opponent is declared the winner.

It may seem strange to begin this chapter with the event that ends the game, but all of the chess strategies ultimately flow from the goal of checkmating your opponent and avoiding checkmate yourself. Every movement, every offensive, and every sacrifice must be made with the same ultimate purpose in mind. To that end, understanding the conditions of victory is essential to understanding all chess strategies, from the opening move to the final moments of the endgame.

Win, Lose, or Draw

While checkmate itself is a static target, there are as many paths to reach it just as there are chess players. Some seek to place constant pressure directly on the enemy king, forcing the opponent to stay on the defensive until they make a fatal error. Others play the long game, picking off enemy pieces until the king is defenseless, or gaining minor positional advantages until their unsuspecting enemy is utterly trapped. Every strategy has its own advantages and complications that arise throughout various stages of play. It's up to you to determine which method is most appealing to your playstyle.

Aggressive players will derive great joy from regularly imposing *check*—the condition under which a king is threatened but can escape by moving away or blocking with another piece. An opponent forced into check has no choice but to respond defensively, making it difficult for them to mount a counterattack. However, this strategy carries a high risk: placing too much focus on an opponent's king may leave you vulnerable to an unforeseen ambush.

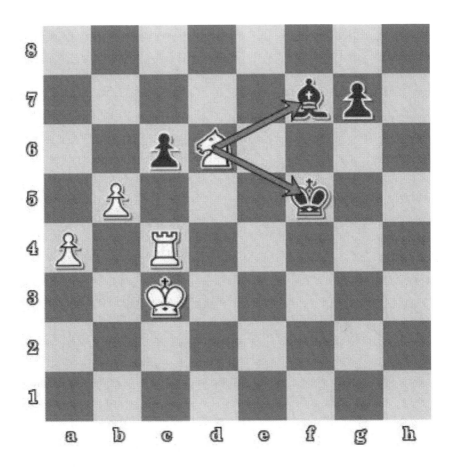

Figure 14: With White's knight imposing check from d6, Black's king must move to a safe location, potentially sacrificing the bishop on f7 in the process. Check can be one of the most effective ways of forcing an opponent to make an unfavorable trade.

More patient players may prefer to slowly reduce an opponent's forces while pursuing a long-term positional advantage. While this strategy generally runs a lower risk in the early and middle games, the longer the game drags on, the more opportunities your opponent may have to force a *stalemate*.

Stalemate occurs when the player whose turn is to play is not in check and has no legal moves available. When a stalemate occurs, the match immediately ends in a draw. This can be especially frustrating if you've spent dozens of moves with an upper hand, only to have your victory swept away and replaced with a draw.

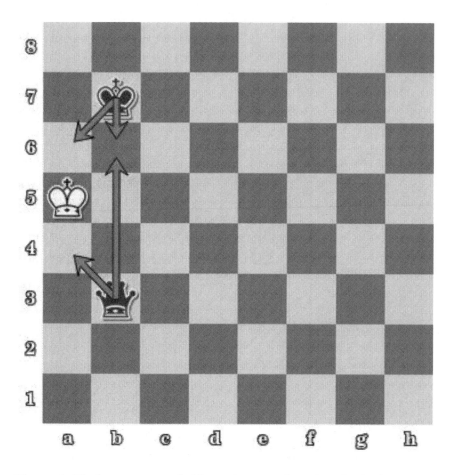

Figure 16: Black may seem to hold an advantage here, but they've let victory slip through their grasp by allowing White to draw in a stalemate since White has no moves available that would not put their king into check.

Apart from a stalemate, draws in chess are exceedingly rare, but not impossible. Conditions under which a draw can occur include the rule of *threefold repetition*, where the same board position has occurred three consecutive times from a particular player in a single match. The *fifty-move rule* is also a condition, in which each player makes 50 moves (total of 100) without a capture or pawn movement, or when a situation arises where checkmate is impossible for either player. Additionally, either player may offer a draw to their opponent at any time during a game. Such an offer can be accepted or declined at the other player's discretion.

Strategy 1: Fool's Mate

Now that you've obtained a thorough understanding of how chess is won and lost, we're ready to dive into the first of several beginner's strategies contained within this book. To begin, let's get acquainted with the fastest possible method of winning a chess game—referred to as *mate in two* or *Fool's Mate*.

While Fool's Mate requires a highly specific set of circumstances and isn't a particularly reliable route to victory, it does illustrate some helpful strategic fundamentals. Learning about it now will also help you avoid falling prey to this common trap laid out to catch beginning players.

To achieve Fool's Mate, you must be playing Black. This is somewhat unusual, as White is generally considered to have a very slight advantage over Black on account of making the first

49

move. However, when White opens with the particularly poor start of f3, Black can attempt to initiate this strategy.

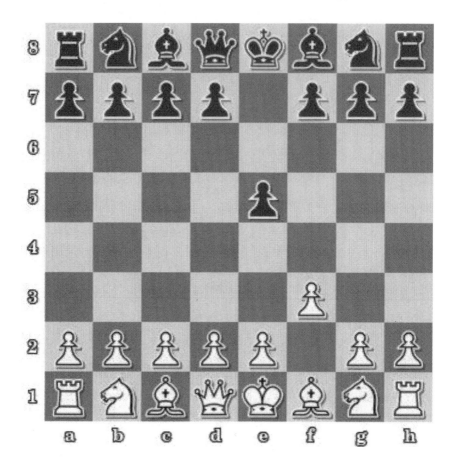

Figure 16: In just a single turn, Black has asserted a strong positional advantage over White. From here, a single blunder from White could seal their fate.

Beyond simply leaving White's king open to attack, f3 is a weak opening move because it fails to provide development opportunities for any piece apart from the king itself. Since the king is relatively weak in the opening anyway, this is a major blunder.

When Black responds at e5, it demonstrates a strong understanding of opening strategy and positional play. From here, Black's kingside bishop and queen can both take to the field immediately. Opening with a pawn towards the center of the board also allows Black to begin setting up a strong defensive wall in the center of the play. Of course, if White makes the mistake of playing g4 next turn, these long-term advantages will cease to matter.

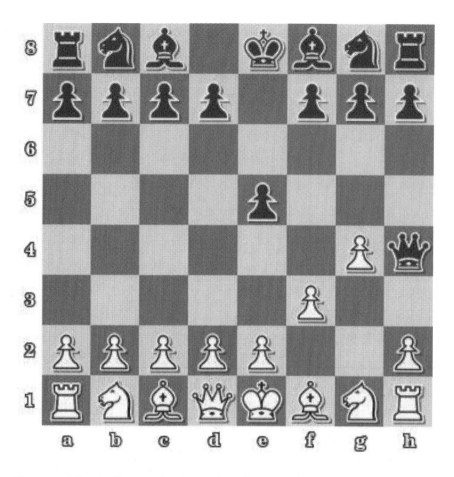

Figure 17: The Fool's Mate has been played to completion. After White moves their pawn to g4 on the second turn, Black responds with a decisive checkmate.

Once again, White has made a blunder on multiple levels. Building a defensive pawn formation on the edges of the board is rarely worth the investment. More importantly, the only piece capable of blocking an attack on the king has given up its ability to do so. Black can easily swoop in with Qh4# to end the game.

While Fool's Mate shows some keen opportunistic play from Black, it's ultimately more of a case study in what not to do from White's perspective. Being caught in this situation can leave a novice player feeling quite embarrassed, but it's simply part of learning the game. Now that you've studied the fastest complete game possible, it's time to examine some deeper chess strategies for different phases of play.

Section 2 – Opening Strategies

The opening ranks begin to mobilize as the pawns start their slow march across the board. Knights take to the field, aiming to thin enemy formations, while bishops begin seeking out the slightest chink in the opposing defense, ready to lash out and escalate the game into an all-out war. The opening game is where strategists begin laying out their elaborate plans, carefully preparing to spring them into action when the time arises.

In technical terms, the opening game is defined as the first few moves of play, where pieces are developed and formations assembled. If that doesn't sound overly specific, it's because it's not. There are no absolute delineations between the phases of a chess game, and often openings and middlegames will overlap.

Chess openings have been studied perhaps more than any other facet of the game, in no small part because many top-level games are won and lost in just the first few moves. Many critical exchanges can take place even in just the first few moves. Even if you're not directly capturing an opponent's piece, shutting down their best-laid plans can establish a dominating positional and mental advantage.

Like any stage of the game, there are boundless ways your opening strategy can take shape. While extreme high-level players study and memorize openings up to dozens of moves, there's no need to be intimidated. While opening strategy is an important aspect of play at any level, it's only one of several stages that make up the full scope of chess strategy.

There are millions of ways a chess game can evolve based on just the first few moves. Still, the most strategically sound openings have been divided into three basic categories: Flank Openings, King's Pawn Openings, and Queen's Pawn Openings. Each of these three categories branches out into dozens of divisions and subdivisions. Still, we'll review just a few of the most popular variations and explore what makes them so effective.

Strategy 2: Openings

King's Pawn Openings

From turn one, White has 20 possible opening moves, and the King's Pawn Opening of e4 is widely considered as one of the most popular and efficient. This may take new players somewhat by surprise, as it seems to leave the king's file exposed to attack.

However, mounting a practical attack on the king remains largely infeasible, especially if White takes advantage of the opportunity to develop both their queen and bishop.

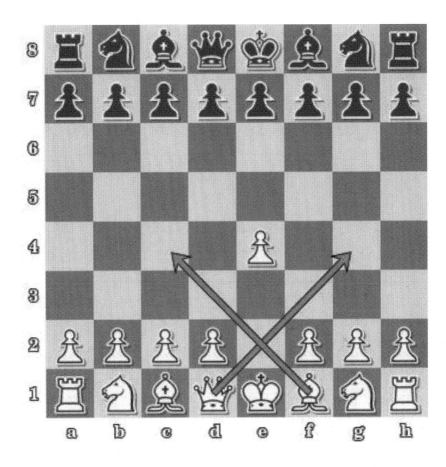

Figure 18: The King's Pawn Opening begins with White's pawn moving to e4. From there, two more powerful pieces can quickly be deployed.

In addition to speeding the development of the queen, e4 is a strong opening because it establishes an early presence at the center of the board. While the downside of this is that White's pawn is temporarily undefended, the player has an opportunity to quickly reinforce it with a robust formation of pawns and harder-hitting pieces.

After such a strong opening, how is Black meant to answer? The most common answer to the King's Pawn Opening is the Sicilian Defense of c5. In fact, this is one of the most common opening exchanges in all of chess. The stark difference in the strategy behind White and Black's opening moves in this scenario perfectly highlights the distinctions of playing as either of the two sides.

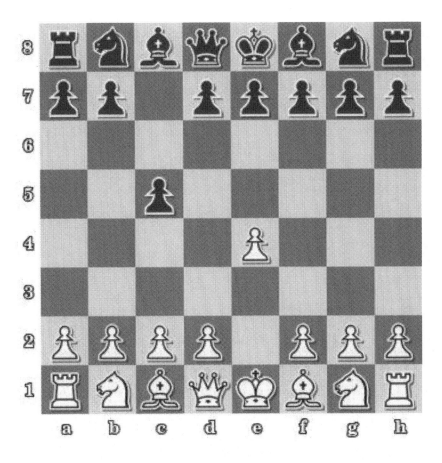

Figure 19: In the Sicilian Defense, unlike White, Black's first move to c5 does little to develop pieces. However, there are other substantial advantages.

Whereas White almost always holds an early lead by holding a default initiative, Black must struggle both to halt White's advantage and seize one of their own. Thus, while White's first move in the King's Pawn Opening focuses on asserting quick dominance and pushing a plan into action, the Sicilian Defense is a more reserved response. Black offers White the opportunity to take control of the kingside files quickly, but in exchange, a powerful phalanx of Black's pawns can dominate the queenside field. If Black acts quickly, they can establish their own zone of control while creating a thorny shield against White's attack.

Alternatively, Black may opt for the even more conservative Caro-Kann Defense, in which the pawn moves only one space to c6. This is generally a move favored by more strategic players who seek to establish a long-term positional advantage and are less concerned with opening exchanges.

Of course, some players prefer direct and immediate confrontation. If dynamic play is more of your style, you might answer the King's Pawn Opening with e5, or an Open Game. White will often answer with Nf3, threatening Black's pawn, to which the most common response is Nc6. From there, White attacks the developed knight with Bb5, creating the Ruy Lopez or Spanish Game.

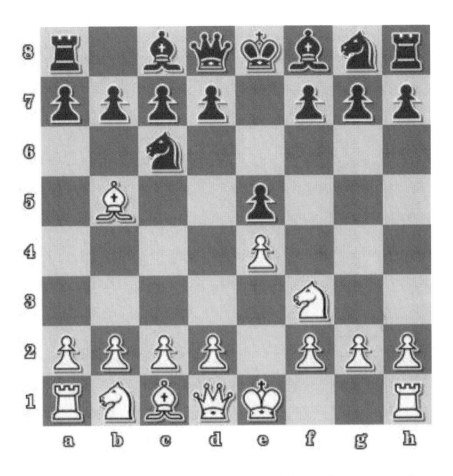

*Figure 20: In the Ruy Lopez opening pictured above, threats are made
quickly, and both players must leap to action.*

One of the fantastic things about the Ruy Lopez is that it offers
several viable moves for both sides at almost every point
throughout the game. In contrast to more formulaic approaches,
Ruy Lopez offers quick-thinking tacticians a veritable buffet line
of attacks and gambits to pursue. In fact, there are so many
different chains of play that can arise from this opening that it has
become one of the most studied phenomena in chess.

While King's Pawn Openings are the most common in high-level play, they're far from the only viable opening strategies. While opening the pawn on the queen's file may not be as popular, it does provide some distinct advantages.

Queen's Pawn Openings

Like the King's Pawn Opening, this opening emphasizes controlling the center of the board from the outset. To begin the game by moving to d4, White prepares to develop the queenside bishop and potentially perform the more difficult queenside castling.

A classic evolution of this opening occurs when black responds with d5, and White proceeds to offer the Queen's Gambit by moving another pawn to c4. Here, Black is faced with a hard decision. They may choose to accept the offered pawn with dxc4, but doing so gives White total control of the center. Alternatively, in denying the bait, Black allows White to pen them in.

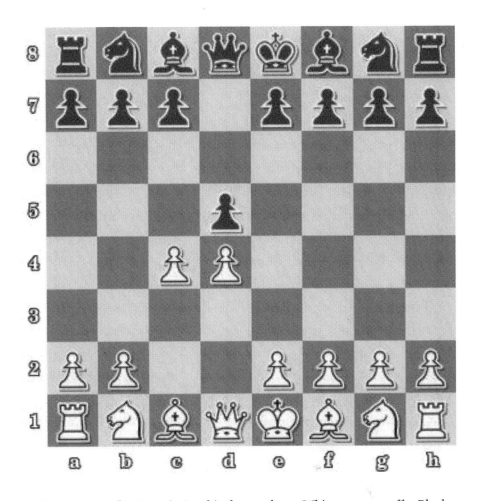

Figure 21: In the Queen's Gambit shown above, White seems to offer Black a pawn, but the gift is poisoned with a difficult choice.

While the Queen's Gambit was extremely popular in the early 20th century, developments in the hypermodern school led to an increasing number of players adopting the Indian Defense and its variations. With this strategy, Black instead opts for the somewhat unusual first-round play of Nf6. Rather than confront White's opening or even attempting to establish their own center of power, Black begins to develop an elaborate web meant to undermine White's supposedly free development.

There are several possible progressions of the Indian Defense, but one of the strongest and most commonly seen in all levels of play is the Nimzo-Indian Defense. In this variation, Black opts to remain flexible for several turns, delaying the building of their own pawn structure with the sole intent of hindering White's.

The standard Nimzo-Indian Defense evolves as such:

1. d4 Nf6

2. c4 e6

3. Nc3 Bb4

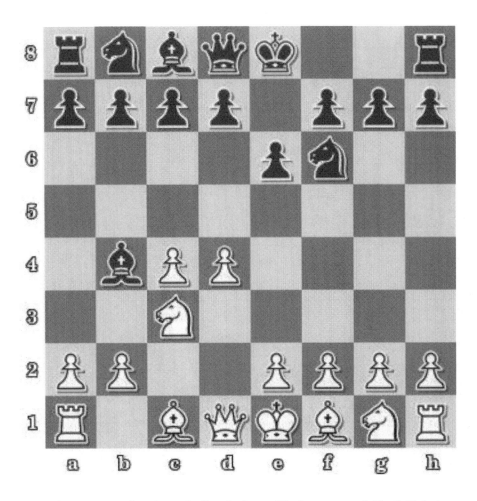

Figure 22: In the Nimzo-Indian Defense, Black opts to quickly field their kingside bishop, knowing it will most likely be sacrificed in due time.

While both the King and Queen's Pawn Openings derive much of their power from establishing a strong presence in the center, there are always other viable options. The final main category of opening, called the Flank openings, seek to exploit the very concept of central control.

Flank Openings

A reference to military flanking maneuvers, in which one force intercepts the other from the side rather than head-on; the Flank openings avoid the center of the board and threaten from the sides. While any number of different opening moves could be considered a Flank opening, the two most common are 1. Nf3, and 1. c4.

The simplest of the two, 1. c4, is often referred to as the English Opening. In addition to the obvious opportunity to field the queen, this opening also gives White several viable strategies to fall back on, making it difficult for Black to counter. For example, White can easily shift back into a Queen's Gambit or advance into the Réti Opening to threaten from both flanks.

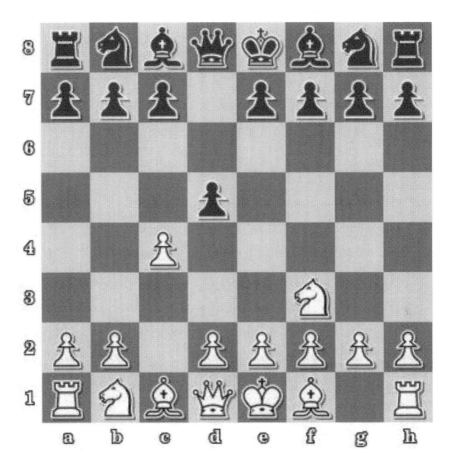

Figure 23: In stark contrast to the King or Queen's pawn openings, the Réti Opening controls the center from outside, rather than within.

The Réti Opening is itself normally played as a progression of the Zukertort Opening—the name given to 1. Nf3. Much like the Indian Defenses, which also emphasize the quick deployment of knights, this opening is a strong example of the hypermodern school of strategy. In contrast to the classical school, which tends to engage in tactical play, hypermodern players tend to be more fluid strategists. The Réti Opening exemplifies their belief that while the center of the board is an important strategic asset, it is controlled most effectively by outside threats rather than a direct confrontation.

Choosing Your Opening

You've familiarized yourself with the four most popular opening moves: 1. e4, 1. d4, 1. c4, and 1. Nf3. You've also learned ways to advance the game from these openings, whether you're playing on Black or White's side. While various masters have theorized on which of these strategies is the strongest, the truth is that no single sequence of moves will allow you to win every game or even most games. If that were the case, chess would almost certainly lose most of its appeal as a pastime!

Rather than searching for an answer on what the "strongest" opening is, ask yourself instead, what openings are most suited to your style of play? Do you prefer straightforward play rooted firmly in tactical prowess? The King's Pawn Openings may serve you well, while the Queen's Pawn Openings and the Queen's Gambit may be of use to those who enjoy a balance of flexibility in direct confrontation. Or, if you're mostly interested in outmaneuvering and out-scheming your opponents, then the Flank openings may be your most enjoyable path to victory.

You'll also need to consider your opponent if you have enough information to do so. If your opponent has you outmatched in raw tactics, consider a slower-paced opening that will allow you to build out a secured strategy before engaging. On the other hand, you might counter a brilliant strategist with an explosive and direct offensive play that prevents them from setting up their elaborate plans. Above all, always try to keep your opponent guessing and on their toes.

The early exchanges of the opening can produce ripples that are felt throughout the game. However, don't assume that losing your first battle means you've lost the war. Likewise, never assume that your opening strategy was so effective that you could begin to let your guard down. A game of chess can turn over on its head with just a few moves.

Unlike the openings and endgames, the middlegame seems to be the least heavily studied area of chess strategy. However, if one thing is true in chess, it's that no detail can ever be overlooked. As you read on, keep these opening strategies in mind, and consider how they can inform your play as we move into the next major phase of play.

Section 3 – Middlegame Strategies

Opposing forces have clashed, opening blows have been exchanged, and kings have retreated to safety as the battle begins to take shape. We're entering the middlegame, perhaps the most poorly understood of the three segments of play. In technical terms, the opening ends, and the middlegame begins when most or all pieces have been developed, and the king has been maneuvered to a more or less secured location, often through castling.

While scholars throughout the ages have dedicated countless hours to analyze openings and endgame scenarios, the middlegame has received relatively little attention. Partly, this is because the middlegame is so dynamic and difficult to predict. Unlike openings, where only selective moves are available until all pieces have been developed, the middlegame often provides players with a plethora of movement options to choose from. Unlike the endgame, where the number of pieces has decreased, players must account for most of their pieces on the field at once. This can be quite overwhelming for both players and chess scholars alike.

In any case, there are very few proper middlegame maneuvers that can be taught through diagrams. Instead, the middlegame strategy comes down to a set of philosophies and tenets. First, each player must keep their king well-guarded. It's not uncommon for a game to end without reaching the endgame at all if checkmate can be achieved earlier.

Second, players should be seeking out every advantage they can leading into the endgame. This can come in the form of superior positioning or material advantage, preferably both. The middlegame may be a transitional phase of play, but how each player comes out of that transition is sure to have a tremendous impact on the outcome.

In this section, we'll go over the fundamentals of achieving these goals. This section may be more abstract than sections on the middle and endgame, but it's nevertheless an important part of understanding the full scope of chess. Indeed, the logic of opening strategy and the basis of the endgame can only be understood through the lens that divides them.

Positioning the King

Some scholars define the endgame as beginning at a point where the king can effectively take on an offensive role in strategy. Keep this goal in mind as you play, but be wary. The middlegame is a dangerous time for a king. With several enemy pieces active on the field at once, the slightest overextension can leave your most valuable piece open to danger. However, that doesn't mean you can't bolster your king's positional advantage while keeping it thoroughly guarded.

Ideally, by the middlegame, you'll have a sturdy formation of pawns protecting the files near your king, with your major and minor pieces ready to fall back to play defense if the need arises. Castling is one of the best ways to achieve this, as it allows you to keep your pawns on the flank you've castled be in the right formation while those in the center play a more active role on the board.

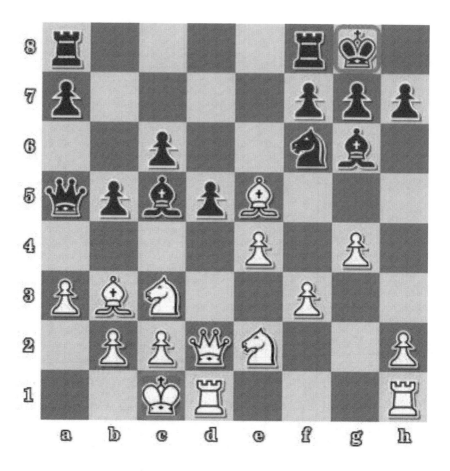

Figure 24: In this early middlegame scenario, each player has castled their king, but otherwise, their strategies are different.

In the figure above, both players have gone to great lengths to secure the king. White has opted for—or been forced into—an extremely defensive formation. While this can provide an effective wall, White runs the risk of being boxed in. Black has taken a more aggressive approach, potentially gaining an advantage if they can maintain the initiative.

Securing Advantages

Assuming your king isn't under threat, the goal of the middlegame is to gain as many endgame advantages as possible. This is done through two primary means, each of which is an intrinsic part of chess strategy: material and board position.

Different masters have differing opinions on which of these is more valuable. Materialists are often more tactical players who value the power and options each piece provides. Positional players tend towards a more detached, strategic outlook, and will sacrifice even valuable material in order to force their opponent into a bad spot. Discovering which type of player you are and why is an important step in finding a comfortable middlegame mindset.

Securing a material advantage means going into the endgame with more *material*—or a higher overall piece value—than your opponent. This is often done through clever gambits, laying traps for the opponent to create scenarios where they're forced to choose which piece to sacrifice. Material gains can be slow to start, but capturing an opponent's queen or rook in the middlegame can speed you to an advantageous endgame.

Positional play is less concerned with targeting individual pieces an opponent controls. Rather, creating an overall favorable spread on the board is this strategy's key to victory. After all, if an opponent's most dangerous pieces can be effectively locked down by your formation, why risk breaking it to capture them? That's not to say positional players are of course more risk-averse. Many will sacrifice a material advantage for the chance to blow a hole through the enemy's guard.

For beginning players, either option is viable, though both extremes should be avoided. The consequences of all-out materialism or positional play can be offset by some masters, but even then, most strive for a balance that leans towards their preferred method.

In either case, learning to make favorable exchanges is perhaps the most important skill to develop and strengthen your middlegame. In formal terms, *exchange* refers to the trading of two pieces, but there are positional exchanges to consider as well. Will you abandon your stranglehold on the center of the board to capture an enemy rook? Your answer may well depend on several other factors in the game, and learning to weigh those factors is what makes for great play in the middlegame.

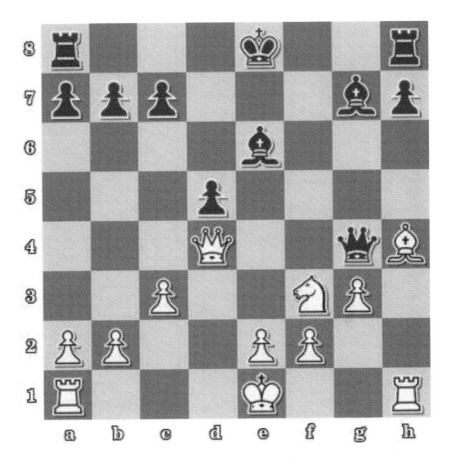

Figure 25: In this scenario, Black has just played Qxg4 and now offers White a hard choice: a potential exchange of queens.

Refer to the diagram above. White can play Qxg4 to capture the enemy queen but will certainly suffer the same fate when Black plays Bxg4. Should White accept Black's offer and exchange queens at this stage?

From a material perspective, White is at a slight advantage, an extra pawn just barely making up the difference for their inferior knight and bishop pair. From a positional standpoint, they also eke out an upper hand over Black, whose pawns are mostly unadvanced and completely unable to protect their exposed king. It would be a gamble, but trading queens here could eliminate a significant wildcard factor from the game and make it easier for White to retain their perilous advantage.

If you're ever unsure whether an exchange is favorable or not, referring back to the valuation system is a good bet. Remember, you usually only want to trade pieces if you're trading a piece of lesser value to capture one of greater value. In some cases, it may be acceptable to trade a knight for a bishop, since bishops are usually more effective in the endgame.

Coming Out on Top

Depending on how the middlegame has gone for you, your perspective on the next phase of play—the endgame—will be drastically different. Players who've outnumbered their opponents secure a solid material advantage, and have a king that's poised and protected can approach this final stage with confidence. Others may not be so lucky. However, the game is never over until it's over.

In the next section, you'll learn how to capitalize on an existing lead to crush your opponents in the endgame as well as how to survive and eke out a comeback victory. If circumstances are truly dire, you'll also learn how to force a draw to save yourself from defeat. As you read on, you can return to this section as many times as needed to review materialistic vs positional play, as these concepts influence every phase of play, despite being most prominent in the middlegame.

Section 4 – Endgame Strategies

The smoke clears across the field of battle, and only a scarce few combatants remain standing on either side. Either both players have executed their middlegame strategies and oppose one another with their favored pieces at the ready, or one player has taken a decisive advantage. It may be a long, brutal hunt before the enemy king is cornered, or it might happen in a single fatal instant. In either case, the endgame is upon them, and only one can win.

As we've already established, phases of play are somewhat malleable, and there's not necessarily a clear indicator of when the endgame begins. In fact, it's not unusual for a king to be checkmated in the middlegame and for the game to close with no endgame at all.

However, a game of chess can be said to have entered its endgame when both players have been reduced to only a few pieces and their kings. Remember, pawns are not considered "pieces" in the technical terms of the game. Often, a pawn's advantage can be the deciding factor in who emerges from the endgame victorious.

In most endgame scenarios, the player who gained a material advantage in the endgame should generally seek to make as many aggressive material trades as possible without sacrificing any pawn. That player's remaining piece(s) can protect pawns on their way to promotion, which is often a death knell for the enemy king. Of course, endgames are extremely varied, and not all of them end with a promoted pawn.

Finally, endgames are characterized by the shift in play where the king becomes a much more powerful offensive tool. Crafty players can weaponize their king to wipe out an opponent's pawn formations or even back the opposing king into a tough spot.

Much like openings, chess endgames are a topic that has been studied extensively throughout the game's history. You can buy dozens of books dedicated to exploring the various endgame scenarios (often called "positions"), many of which feature theoretical exercises that allow students of the game to test their wit and skill. In this guide, we'll focus mainly on the various types of endgames and what beginners need to know to achieve checkmate in each of them.

Endgames Without Pawns

Because of the importance of pawns in the endgame, many players will attempt to eliminate the threat of enemy promotion by wiping their opponent's pawns out entirely. This results in some endgames where there are no remaining pawns at all.

In these scenarios, a king and either a queen or a rook can easily achieve a checkmate against an opponent. Paired bishops on opposite colors also have a fairly simple time achieving checkmate. A bishop and knight will have a much more difficult time, and with two knights, it is nearly impossible to checkmate an opponent, especially if they have a few pieces remaining on the board.

The primary threat in an endgame with no remaining pawns is the possibility of an opponent forcing a draw through a stalemate. Ironically, this becomes somewhat easier for a king pitted against a king and queen, especially if the player with more material is less experienced. Due to the queen's vast range of threatened squares, a wily player can slip their king into position for a stalemate.

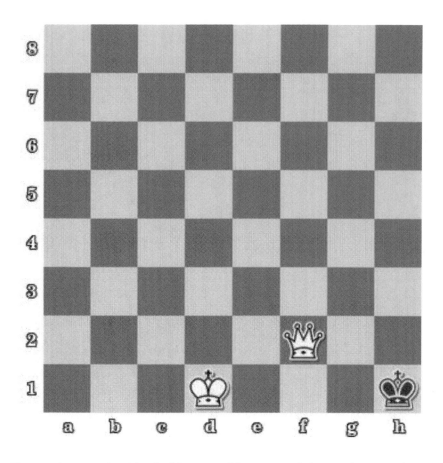

Figure 26: Assuming it's Black's move, this game ends in a stalemate. This is undoubtedly a frustrating prospect for the dominant player.

Fortunately, this type of stalemate is usually easy to avoid once you've become aware of it. Simply remain aware of where your opponent can move on their next turn and ensure there's always at least one safe square available.

Another major factor in endgames with very few pieces, like those discussed here, is the concept of *opposition*. Opposition occurs when two kings are separated from each other only by one rank or file. In this scenario, the player whose turn it is to move has no choice but to move their king away from the enemy, assuming the king is the only piece they can move.

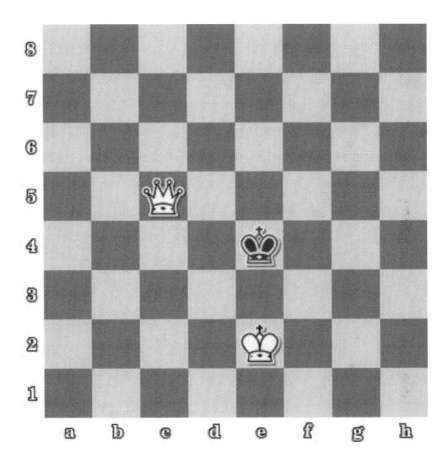

Figure 27: Assuming Black's turn to move, White's king uses opposition to effectively threaten the three squares directly in front of it, cutting off almost half of Black's options for movement and forcing them into an increasingly difficult position.

Opposition can be a decisive factor in nearly every endgame scenario, but it plays an especially critical role in endgames without pawns and—ironically—endgames with only pawns.

King and Pawn Endgames

Sometimes an endgame results in all pieces being captured on both sides, leaving only the kings and their remaining pawns. More than any other endgame, having more pawns than your opponent is key to victory in these scenarios, especially if you have passed pawns on their way to promotion.

In any case, precision is key in a king and pawn endgame, and this becomes truer with the fewer pawns that are remaining on the board. The classic king and pawn vs king endgame have been analyzed endlessly by strategists for this very reason. In such a contest, a single error can turn a win into a draw or a draw into a loss.

In a king and pawn vs king endgame, each player's objective becomes clear: the player with the pawn must promote it to achieve checkmate, while the lone king must prevent that outcome in order to secure a draw. To do so, the lone king must either capture the enemy pawn or occupy the square directly in front of that pawn or the square in front of that. By doing so, the lone king can simply cycle through positions to keep the game going indefinitely without the pawn progressing, thereby forcing a draw.

Figure 28: So long as Black plays without error, this game could continue forever. Black has succeeded in forcing a draw.

In these scenarios, where success or failure rides on every single movement, the concept of *triangulation* is essential for both parties. Basically, triangulation in chess refers to the ability of a piece (almost always the king) to return to the same position in three moves. Usually, triangulation also refers to the tactic in which this maneuvering is used to gain a positional advantage over the opponent.

Triangulation can be a tricky concept to grasp in the abstract. To better understand it, let's refer back to the diagram above, but with a few added visual aides.

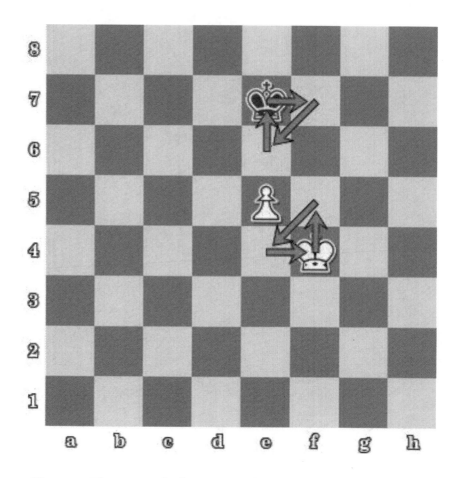

Figure 29: The reason Black can successfully force a draw is because of triangulation.

In this scenario, Black's king must prevent the pawn from progressing, and White's king must remain within one square of the pawn to protect it as it advances. As long as Black continuously cycles through Ke7, Kf7, and Ke6—and always counters White's Kf5 with Kf7—Black will succeed at forcing a draw through the use of triangulation and opposition.

However, if Black isn't properly triangulating, White can also use the same concepts to win. If White can reach a position on Kf5 and Black makes the mistake of responding with Ke7, White will have gained a fatal upper hand. White's pawn can finally advance to e6 while still being protected by its king, and Black will have no choice but to retreat. This is the only scenario in which a long king can still lose when controlling the two squares directly in front of the final pawn in this type of endgame.

In this scenario, Black would likely have preferred not to make a move at all, and simply hold their blocking position indefinitely. However, the rules of chess mandate that each player must move one piece each round. The idea that a player might be forced to move even when it's against their best interests is called *zugzwang*. It's a concept that permeates chess and many other turn-based games, but it's particularly important in chess endgames.

Like that of opposition, triangulation and *zugzwang* are both key concepts to be aware of in any endgame strategy. Not only are they individually important tactical tools, when used together, they also turn your king into an offensive powerhouse capable of turning the tide as the game draws to a close. Now that you've been introduced to all three, you're ready to study some of the other possible endgame scenarios. As you read on, try to think about strategic roles your king could play in each possible endgame.

King and Knight Endgames

The knight is the most difficult piece to deliver checkmate with, since its features are relatively few during endgames, as many players choose to exchange theirs during the middlegame. While a knight can't deliver checkmate on its own, it can work well in tandem with other pieces. Since you can never be sure when you might be forced to enter the endgame leaning heavily on a remaining knight, it's best to understand their endgame strategy, even if it isn't optimal.

Against pawns, a knight's primary objective is to use its jumping ability to weave through enemy blockades and pick off pawns one at a time. A passed pawn can be a nuisance, but the knight should be able to block it, if not capture it before it can promote.

Unfortunately, relying on a knight to stand against rooks, queens, or even bishops often means you're aiming to draw rather than win. The good news is, knights are much more capable defenders in the endgame than they are attackers. By keeping your knight and king close to one another, both pieces can work in tandem to support one another, making it easy enough to draw against a stronger piece like a rook.

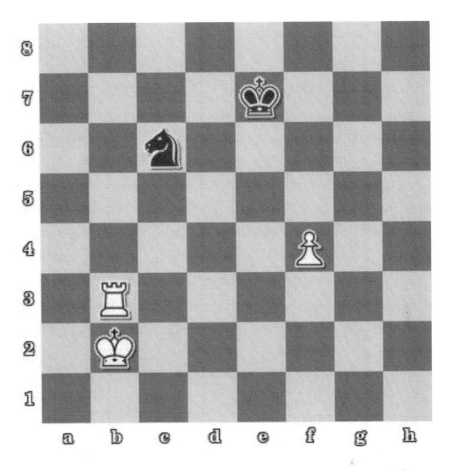

Figure 30: This is a difficult endgame for Black, but not impossible.

In the figure above, Black must stop the advance of the enemy pawn if they're to force a draw. Black's knight will have difficulty capturing the passed pawn, but it can easily block and provide defensive cover while the Black king moves to capture. If the player can pull this off, Black will successfully draw by keeping the king and knight close together and able to protect one another.

With just a few more pieces in play, the knight's defensive capabilities become more of an asset. Even two knights can protect each other and the king well enough to force a draw, if not significantly outnumbered. Still, the knight is generally not a preferred piece to be brought into the endgame and should be sacrificed in favor of a more powerful offensive weapon if possible.

King and Bishop Endgames

While certainly a more versatile attacker in the endgame than a knight, a lone bishop remains incapable of forcing checkmate. With a pair of bishops, this becomes significantly more manageable, since they're both on opposite-colored squares.

One notorious endgame scenario is when each player has only a bishop and pawns remaining, but the bishops are on opposite colors. Since the bishops cannot attack each other, they must be used primarily as defensive tools to support the players' remaining pawns. This is one of the few cases where a "bad" bishop penned in by surrounding pawns is actually an advantage, as it can provide superior protection.

Bishops are also known for being involved in one of the most common pawnless endgames: a rook and bishop versus one rook. In this scenario, the player with the material generally wins by using the bishop to chase the defender's rook away from squares that allow it to protect its king. With this done, the attacker's rook and king can corner the enemy and achieve a checkmate.

A common counter to this that allows the materially weaker player to draw is the Cochrane Defense. Named from the chess master John Cochrane, the defending player uses the rook to effectively pin the bishop to its king near the center of the board. With only the enemy's rook left as a credible threat, the defender can often force a draw.

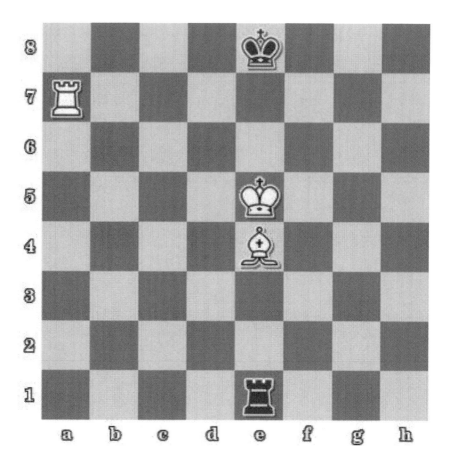

Figure 31: From this position (the Cochrane Defense), Black can endlessly stall out the game with a bit of clever play.

Ultimately, unless they're paired together, bishops are supporters in the endgame, not attackers. As we move on to the more aggressive role of the major pieces in the final game, keep in mind how knights and bishops can be used to support these more powerful pieces if you find yourself with any of these remaining pieces as the game draws to a close.

King and Rook Endgames

Rook endgames are among the most common and best studied endgames. This is partly because they are always being late to develop and are quite valuable; rooks are not generally exchanged until very late in the game. Another factor is that rook endgames can be extremely complex. On an open board, a rook can generally lock out any rank or file combination in a matter of two moves, often less. This makes pawn promotion much more difficult than in endgames featuring mostly minor pieces.

Especially in a rook and pawn endgame, positioning your rook on the seventh rank can spell doom for your opponent. There are no guarantees, but a rook that controls the seventh rank can sweep up undeveloped pawns while protecting its advancing allies. A famous example comes from the 1924 contest between Jose Raul Capablanca and Savielly Tartakower. In this match, Capablanca successfully infiltrated the enemy lines with his rook leading into the endgame. After a fairly even contest, Tartakower was defenseless against this sudden threat.

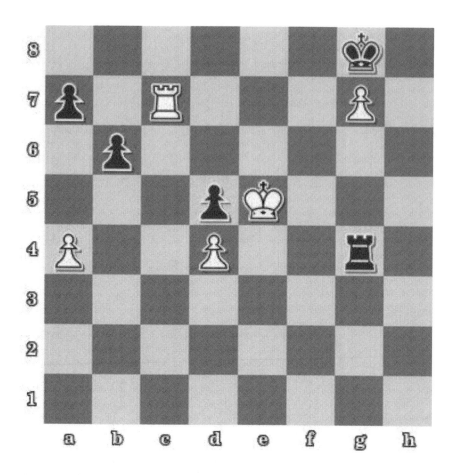

Figure 32: Materially, this endgame may seem dead even, but White's Rook is far better positioned to provide an overwhelming advantage.

Take the diagram above as an example. Assuming Black is to move, they're faced with two equally disastrous options, all thanks to White's rook. They could continue holding back White's pawn with the king, but White's rook will continue to wreak havoc on their pawns. Or, Black could capture the pawn on g7 with their rook, which almost certainly ends with a rook exchange. While

Black would end that exchange with one additional pawn, White's king is still far better positioned to support its fewer pawns on their way to promotion. Black almost certainly loses this match.

This is the general principle behind rook endgames—aggression. The rook must seek to wipe out as much enemy material as possible, both to gain a material advantage and increase its mobility.

King and Queen Endgames

Despite its tremendous power, the queen appears in a significantly lower number of endgames than the rook. This may be because queens tend to be more active in the middlegame than the rooks, generally having the side-effect of them being exchanged or otherwise captured before the endgame can begin. Another reason is that due to the queen's ability to overwhelm the enemy while active on the board, many games where the queen is not captured come to an end before a proper endgame can be declared.

If you do hold onto your queen into the endgame, it's a powerful asset. Even on its own, the queen can easily work in tandem with your king to force checkmate. As with a rook, however, the goal of your queen coming into the endgame should be to eliminate any pesky pawn—especially passed pawns—that your opponent still controls. The limitations of a queen are perhaps the best illustration of how important the king and pawns become in the endgame.

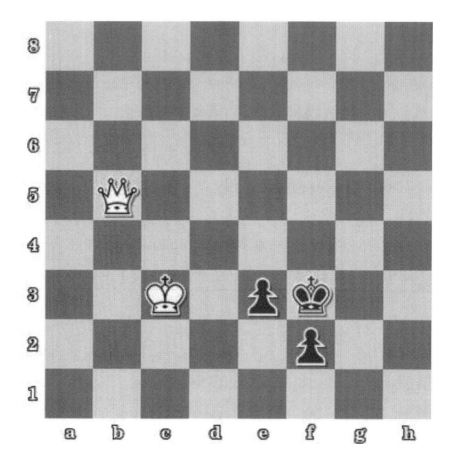

Figure 33: Despite the massive material imbalance, Black still has many paths leading to victory since it already has two passed pawns close to being promoted.

In the figure above, Black has created a strong *fortress*—a formation of pieces that both defend the king and allow the king to defend them. White would have a bout of difficult play ahead even if Black's pawns were still further back, but their position on the second and third ranks makes this situation truly dire. As long as Black keeps a strong formation, White cannot capture without losing their queen, and may as well lose the game. Due to White's poor positioning, Black is likely to be victorious here.

Part of the problem is that in this example, the White king and queen are not positioned to support each other. White's best option is for the king to move to d4 and attempt to capture on e3, but by then, Black will have a promoted pawn defended by its king, and the match becomes materially even.

A far better example of the king and queen working in tandem comes from the 18th-century player François-André Danican Philidor. With both an opening and endgame position named for him, Philidor's contributions to chess analysis are quite weighty.

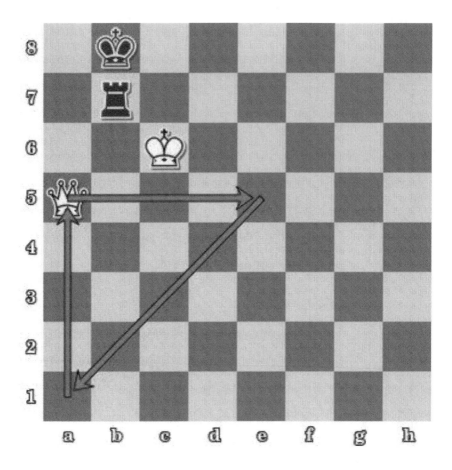

Figure 34: Here, White's King and Queen are working in perfect sync, forcing black into zugzwang *if needed, and securing a victory.*

In this position, analyzed by Philidor, Black is experiencing *zugzwang* if they're to move, their rook forced to abandon its king and weaken both of their positions. If White is to move, they can easily force Black into the same state of *zugzwang* by triangulating with the queen, keeping Black's king in constant check during the process.

Make no mistake—the queen is a fantastic asset in any endgame. However, if there's one thing to learn from this section, it's that positional advantages make more of a difference in the endgame than in any other phase. A poorly positioned queen is easily thwarted by two well-placed pawns, after all.

But what about the human element? We've weighed material factors and positional factors, but if that were all there was to it, chess would be a rather boring game. The truth is, no scenario ever has a truly predestined outcome.

Endgame Theory vs Reality

Some of the earliest documentation we have on chess analysis has to do with endgame studies. It's a topic that's been analyzed back and forth endlessly over generations of expert players. Today, computer analysis has brought this field of study to new heights, with online databases called tablebases enabling theorists to review exhaustive analysis of endgame positions.

With so much scholarship on the subject, many guides you might refer to will show you a position on the board and state simply that White is sure to win in a certain number of moves. The critical element to remember here is that such declarations assume perfect play on both sides. Two queens *can* certainly outmaneuver a queen in the endgame, but few actual players are also likely to possess the skill to do so too.

Assuming you're playing against others of your skill level, don't be discouraged by high-level theory. These complex scenarios are often meant to illustrate unusual and extreme cases and shouldn't be something you expect to encounter. While master-level players might attempt to reverse-engineer these specific scenarios, for us, they're theoretical illustrations of key concepts that can have a more practical effect on endgame strategy.

By combining your knowledge of key endgame tactics— opposition, triangulation, fortresses, and *zugzwang*, you'll stand a much better chance in an endgame scenario. On top of that, you're now equipped to circle back and apply what you know about all three phases of the game to each other. From setting up in the opening to exchanging in the middlegame, you now possess the tools needed to formulate your own comprehensive chess strategies.

Of course, just like endgame analysis, a study can only ever take you so far. Now that you have the tools, it's time to start putting them into action.

The Principles of Chess Openings

There is a huge number of chess opening examples out there. There are common openings and there are unique openings. But as we had said earlier chess is a very dynamic game and what seems like a familiar game might go so many ways. One single different move can change the entire game. What you don want to do is cram an opening move. Studying and familiarizing yourself with opening moves is a good strategy. Using some of these moves can be a good idea too but not always. Don't forget that your opponent has also studied these moves and he can easily spot the fact that you are replicating a common move and use that to your advantage. You might also have a terrible memory and you forget what happens after what. Lastly, there is also the fact that the enemy may choose to make a statistically unlikely move that doesn't necessarily fit in your plan.

The best thing to do is to understand the principles behind chess opening moves. The various both common and unique openings all seek to serve the same purpose hence there is a need to understand them.

Chapter 6:   Principles of chess openings

1. Center Control

By now from the objectives you may have established just how important center control is to one's position in a chess game. For this reason, most opening plays start by opening up the center pawns and trying to get pieces especially knights and bishops to the center. It is very unlikely and highly advised against to make an opening using the flank pawns. This serves no clear objective at the beginning of a game.

The most common openings in chess matches start with the **e** and **d** file pawns. The white **e2** to **e4** is the most likely to occur opening and after that, it depends on black's reaction.

2. Knight Preference

In openings, preference by most advanced players is given to knights over bishops. After opening up the first pawns probably the king and queen, the bishops have a clear path of development. So, preference is given to knights. You first develop the knight towards the center before moving to the bishops.

3. Castle Side

While developing both the knight and bishop castle side is a very important thing to consider. Castling, especially earlier in the game is are important in protecting the king and avoiding nuisance checks or a surprise checkmate caused by a blocked king. Deciding between castling kingside or queenside helps you decide on the bishop and knight to develop first hence creating the room you would eventually require to castle.

4. King Safety

Once you have castled you will be sitting protected for a while so long as there are pawns blocking a direct path to you. Openings are very much influenced by the level of king safety. All pawns covering the king are kept away from the openings and the local area covered by the king is not left exposed. Also, in your opening, it is never advisable to shift your king from the first rank. If your king leaves the first rank as early as during openings your chances of losing go very high.

5. Rook File Freedom

A rook is a very powerful piece on the board. However, if not properly developed it can underperform and lose material advantage. In the opening, you need to secure a free file for the rooks as soon as possible. A rook with a fully open file poses a direct threat across to the enemy side.

6. Multiple Pieces

When opening you need to make sure that you play with a pawn or piece just once unless necessary. If you have to play with the same on multiple occasions it keeps you from developing your other pieces and gives your opponent the freedom and time to conquer the center. A good opening is one that forces the opponent to retreat a piece giving you a chance to develop with an advantage.

Keep in mind that a good opening can be very instrumental in guaranteeing to attain all the objectives first. And in eventuality winning the match.

Chapter 7:   Earn The Center

The center in chess refers to the four innermost squares on the chessboard and also the immediate surrounding squares. Having control over the center in a chess game is of utmost importance. Centrally places pieces have more flexibility and wield more power in a game. Take for example in the case of a knight. Compare a knight situated at the side and a knight situated in the center. The knight on the side loses the ability to cover some extra squares in terms of movement. He can only move toward the inside whereas the knight at the center can move in all directions.

Pieces and pawns covering the center pose a bigger threat to the opponent as one piece is able to place multiple roles while in the center as compared to any other point in the board. This goes a long way into facilitating your material advantage and guarantees proper piece development. Achieving central control is not an easy task especially when playing a more advanced opponent as they are fully aware of the need to control the center and also play towards the same goal. So how do you get to control the center before the other person does so?

When starting the game, you should consider the center as a goal. Viewing it as a goal on its own enables you to focus your attention on getting there. You cannot have divided attention when trying to control the center as your opponent won't make the same mistake. You need to give it your whole at first. This doesn't mean that you completely ignore all the aspects of the game. Keep in mind that chess is a game of very many possible moves and not keeping an eye on the entire board or the objectives of your opponent can be costly. Focus, but don't focus too much on one thing that you ignore the bigger picture.

Move your pieces towards the center at all times unless there is a reason not to. If you are threatened on the flank side deal with that. If a piece is playing a role on the outer files and ranks it's okay to let it keep doing so. Develop as many pieces towards the center as you can. When it comes to dealing with the fact that both of you are targeting the same thing, that is the center. This means that you won't just find empty squares. There will be pieces already in the square or heading towards the center. Your task here will be to keep them from doing so. Chase their pieces away from the center. Apply as much pressure as you can to ensure they opt-out. When it comes to pawns you need to keep in mind the two locational values of the pawns. Flank vs Center pawns. When the opportunity presents itself always make sure to exchange center located pawns for flanks.

In other cases, you may have enemy pieces who aren't located at the center but are posing a threat to the center. For example, a directly open bishop that has access to an entire long diagonal. Or a knight that can get to the center with one move. These are the ones you should target first when mounting attacks. Taking out these pieces enables you to occupy the center unchallenged. This is very important as getting to the center and then turning to play defensive roles can be a serious waste of strategic positioning.

Always remember that central pieces are the best-developed pieces. These pieces have control of a large number of squares on the board. While at the center a piece can be a defender, an attacker, or even a restrictor. These pieces also have the ability to escape danger easily and quickly with single moves as they have multiple options in terms of direction. Having a piece at the center can be good at posing danger or mounting a double defense. A bishop controlling a long diagonal can defend on one end and then slide directly to do the same on the opposite side of the board without having to lose its dominance on the board.

Chapter 8: Basic Techniques For Defending and Attacking

A typical chess game involves attacking your opponent's pieces and defending your own pieces. Your major aim of attacking your opponent's pieces is to gain a chance to checkmate his king.

Your major aim of defending your own pieces is to have enough powerful pieces that can defend your own king, seeing as the king is one of the less powerful pieces on the board.

Additionally, when playing chess, it is not just about attacking and defending pieces; you have to consider the quality of the pieces you are attacking and defending. It is foolish to lose your queen while protecting your pawn. So, it is more of a game of quality than quantity. Yes, having pieces on your side can help you protect your king, but nothing beats having powerful pieces, even if they are just a few.

So, before you make a move, you have to pause, think, and judge the move critically. You will need to ask yourself, what do I stand to gain or lose with this move? Will this move open up my king or any of my other pieces to attack? Will this move help me to weaken my enemy's defense? These and more are some of the questions that should always go through your mind when you are considering making a move.

The Mobility of Pieces on an Empty Board

Even though you have seen how the different pieces move on an empty board, we want to refresh your memory by revisiting the topic.

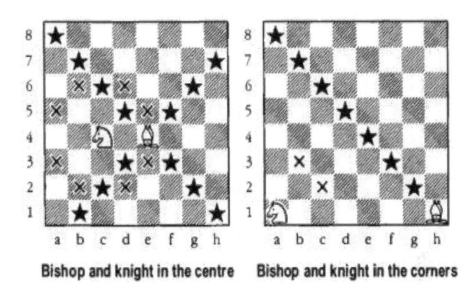

Bishop and knight in the centre   Bishop and knight in the corners

Most chess pieces perform better and wield more power when they are in the center of the board than anywhere else. When a piece sits in the center, there are a lot of squares that the piece in particular can move to.

In the first diagram shown above, you can see that the knight and bishop are occupying a central position on the board. The stars drawn on the board shows the number of squares that the bishop controls. The cross drawn on the board shows the different squares that the knight's control from its central position. The bishop easily controls 13 squares while sitting on the 4e-square while the knight controls eight.

In the second diagram, we have moved the knight and the bishop to the first rank. Again, we used stars to show the number of squares that the bishop controls and crosses to show the number of squares that the knight controls.

As you can see, the number of squares that the two pieces control has reduced drastically, and it was simply due to a change of position. While on the first rank, the knight controls only two squares, and the bishop controls only seven.

Comparing the mobility of different pieces

Piece	Centre Moves	Edge Moves	Corner Moves	Reduction in Mobility
Rook	14	14	14	0%
Queen	27	21	21	22%
Bishop	13	7	7	46%
King	8	5	3	63%
Knight	8	4	2	75%

The table shown above illustrates the number of squares that a chess piece can control when the piece is making a center move and when the piece is moving from the edge. The values shown above are only attainable if the board is empty, so we are assuming an empty board.

When you look closely at the figures, you will notice that the rook is rarely affected by position. Whether it is at the end, center, or at a corner, the rook will still be able to control 14 squares on an empty board. The queen's location on the board affects the number of moves the piece can make, although the difference is not much.

The bishop is one piece that loses much of its strength or power when it is not in the center of an empty board. Once a bishop finds himself at the edge of the board, the number of squares he can control reduces from 13 to 7, a significant number.

The most affected piece among all is the knight. When in a center position on an empty board, the knight can move to 8 different squares, but when the piece is in a corner, he can only move to two squares.

Giving Pieces a Numerical Value

Piece	Value
Queen	9
Rook	5
Bishop	3
Knight	3
Pawn	1
King	not relevant

In chess, it is important to recognize that all pieces are not equal in strength. This will help you when attacking and defending pieces, so you don't lose a powerful piece while trying to defend a less powerful one.

The figures above show the almost universally accepted numerical values of each chess piece. Since the king cannot be captured or traded in a game, it doesn't have an assigned numerical value or strength.

As expected, the queen is the most powerful piece on the board, with a numerical value of 9. The pawn, as seen earlier, is the lowliest of the pieces, with only a numerical value of 1.

When you look at these values, it is easy to see that the queen is worth about a rook, a bishop, and a pawn. The worth of a knight can be equated to the worth of three pawns. A single rook can be equated to two pawns and a knight or bishop.

It is important to state that the value of a chess piece might change depending on the position of the piece on the board. For instance, when trapped in a locked position, the knight will have more value than the rook. But in an open board or position, the rook will definitely be more valued than the knight.

Safe Moves

In chess, a safe move is simply one that doesn't give your opponent the chance to gain material advantage. Learning how to make safe moves is one of the fundamental skills you must acquire as a chess player. Remember, your opponent is always out to attack, weaken your defenses, and checkmate your king, and it is your job to stop that from happening.

One thing you should try to avoid when playing is allowing your piece to be captured for no return. If your piece must be captured, make sure you capture your opponent's own that is of equal or higher value. When most beginners are playing, they mostly allow their pieces to be captured for no return. In chess, this is referred to as leaving your pieces "en prise."

Here are the two most important questions you must always ask yourself when making a move with a piece:

1. If I move this piece now, can it be captured by my opponent's piece?

2. If I move this piece, will it open up my other pieces to be captured or attacked?

While these two important questions can help you make safer moves, they don't tell the entire story.

Making Safe Moves #1

White to play

In the above diagram, it is the turn of White to play. Let's look at some possible moves he can make.

1 Nf4 and 1 Ne5 are perfectly safe moves as there are no threats to the knights in those new squares. Also, the moves will not open up White's other pieces to attack.

Now, if White plays 1 Nb4, you can see that it is an unsafe move. Why is it unsafe? The enemy pawn on c5 can capture the knight. If that happens, it means that White sacrificed a powerful knight for no return at all.

If White plays 1 Qe4 and 1 Qd5, then they are safe moves. However, if White plays 1 Qc6, then that's an unsafe move. It is unsafe because the enemy queen on c8 can capture the queen on c6.

White to play

Playing 1 h4 will be seen as a complex move because the pawn can be attacked and captured by the enemy bishop on e7. But then, white will be able to retaliate by using the g3-pawn to capture the enemy bishop on h4.

When speaking materially, White will gain three points from the above move and lose just one. So, the 1 h4 move can be considered a safe one. How did White gain three points? Because he captured an enemy's bishop, while the enemy only captured White's pawn. Remember that the bishop's numerical value is 3 while the pawn's numerical strength is 1. So, White only lost one point and gained 3.

Safe Moves #2

White to play

In the diagram shown above, it is White's turn to play. If White plays 1 Nd4, what will happen? Black will use his rook on d8 to capture the knight (1... Rxd4). White can recapture Black's rook by playing 2 Qxd4.

Speaking materially, this move makes White lose a knight (which is 3 points) and gains five points because it captured an enemy's rook, which has a numerical value of 5. So, the material "balance" of that move made by White is 2. i.e., (5 minus 3 = 2). So, 1 Nd4 is a safe move.

If White had played 1 Qd4, then that would not be a safe move. The reason is that Black will retaliate by playing 1 Rxd4. Then White would make a second move by playing 2 Nxd4. This move is not safe because White gained 5 points but lost 9, incurring a loss of 4 points.

Finally, 1 b4 is yet another unsafe move. The reason is that even though the pawn moved cannot be captured by an opponent, White has by that move left the a4-pawn undefended – and it can be captured by either the enemy bishop or rook.

Threatening Your Opponent's Pieces

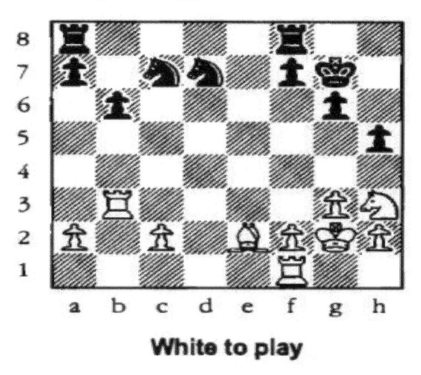

White to play

It is not just enough to learn how to make safe moves; to win a chess game, you will need to know how to threaten or attack your opponent's pieces. This doesn't mean you should attack blindly – just like safe moves, you have to make calculated attacks that wouldn't see you losing more points than you gain.

In the diagram shown above, it is White's turn to play. If White wants to attack the undefended black knight on d7, he can move in four possible ways. See if you can spot the four possible ways.

If White plays 1 Rd1 or 1 Rd3, those are safe moves. If White plays 1 Bb5, that's also a safe move. If White plays 1 Bb5, Black can capture the bishop using a knight by playing 1... Nxb5. White will have to recapture b5 using a rook by playing 2 Rxb5. For this particular move, the overall material gain/loss is zero.

The fourth possibility of attacking the d7-knight will involve White playing 1 Bg4. But that's not a safe move as White could easily reply with 1... hxg4. After this move, White would lose 3 points. So, it cannot be considered to be a safe threat.

Chapter 9:   Models And Methods Of Ckeckmating

In a chess recreation, you ought to take a look at the opposite king. It will help you practice the elements because of the loading agent.

Thanks to this guide, you may enhance your vision at the chessboard, and you may discover spouses faster.

Anastasia's spouse is a general manner to test. The officer took his name from the radical Anastasia und das Schachspiel by means of Johann Jakob Wilhelm Heinz. It is executed the usage of a knight and a crusher to trap and take a look at the black king.

Andersen's Colleague

Andersen's wife is a well-known manner to test and is known as Adolf Anderson. This officer uses a white rook or a queen to check the black king.

The boot is supported using a pedestrian or a bishop. Anderson's wife is frequently visible before, and very little can be finished to save her.

Arab Neighbor

The wife of Saudi Arabia is a general way to test. The verification officer works with the knight so that the king's diagonal squares are black, so he can capture him with a rook to prepare the check. This dealer can test the rank or report.

The Player Behind the Rank

The back pair is a fashionable manner to test. It takes place that a collar or queen controls a king who is blocked through his thick (mainly pedestrian) pieces inside the first or eighth row, and there is virtually no manner to carry the attacking piece to the troubled king. For example, the Black Queen cannot capture the white rook.

Bishop and Knight of the Maidana

The bishop and knight officer is a well-known way to check. It takes place that the king and his thick pieces pressure the bishop and knight, the king of the adversary, at the nook of the photo that the bishop can manipulate so that he can deliver his spouse. It is also possible to use urgent the missing king in the deadlock, in which he can be checked.

However, of the four critical missions, along with Queen Kate, Box Matt and King, and the 2 suspicious purposes of the bishops, that is a part of the husband's hardest strengths, as he can play 34 full-sport games. Sometimes the result is a draw.

Blackburn's Wife

Blackburn's spouse is known as Joseph Henry Blackburn and is an unusual way to check. Using a black liquor (in place of a bishop or queen), the Czech officer restricts the getaway of the black king in square f8. One of the bishops restricts the motion of the black king by using lengthy operating distances, while the knight and bishop work nearby. Blackburn's spouse's threats may be used to weaken Black's function.

Matt Field

Matt Box is a part of the 4 most important missions with the queen's spouse, the king, and the 2 bishops of the bishops and bishops and knights. It occurs like the king's side and the king's pavement container empty to the corner or the aspect of the plank.

Corner Couple

A corner couple is a popular manner to test. It is executed by locking the king in a nook using a rook and a queen and using a knight to lease the managing officer.

Cosio's Wife

Cosio's spouse is a fashionable manner to test. The checkmate is an inverted model of Dovetail's husband. It became named after an observation conducted in 1766 by Carlo Cosio.

Similar to Bishop Damiano

Bishop Damiano is an incredible direction to verify. The verification officer makes use of the queen and the bishop, wherein the bishop is used to support the queen, and the queen is conversant in engaging inside the mission. The checkmate is named after Pedro Damiano.

Damiano's Colleague

Damiano's wife is an excellent way to check one of the oldest. It is executed with the aid of closing the king on the floor and using a queen to begin the concluding blow. This rook can also be a bishop or queen.

Damiano's wife regularly comes by sacrificing a collar in report H, then examines the king with the queen in report h, then goes after his wife. Pedro Damiano first posted the Czech agent in 1512. In Damiano's publications, he did not put the white king on the board, which led to his failure to enter many chess databases due to the refusal to accept illegal positions.

The Wife of David and Goliath

David and Goliath's wife is a fashionable way to test. Although David and Goliath's husband can take quite a few forms, they are generally known as the husband in which the infantry is the closing attacking piece, and the enemy's infantry is positioned nearby.

Same Color as Double Bishop

Binary doubling is an ideal way to test. It's like being a wife, but a little easier. The inspector includes the assault on the king, the usage of two bishops, and, consequently, the king is located in the back of a black pedestal that has now not been moved.

Columbofil Colleague

Dovetail's spouse is a preferred way to check. It includes overthrowing the darkish king in the version displayed on the right-hand facet. It doesn't make a difference how the sovereign is upheld; it doesn't make a distinction which of the other pieces is dark as a knight.

Epaulette's Spouse

Epaulet, or Epaulet mate, by way of its genuine definition, is an inspection agent in which parallel retreat squares are drawn for a king, occupying parts of it and stopping it from escaping. Epaulette's most everyday spouse consists of the king inside the lower back row, stuck among rooks. The visual resemblance among the rooks and the bulbs, the ornamental portions of the shoulder worn over the army uniforms, give it the name of the sheet.

Greco's Colleague

Greek spouses are a fashionable way to test. This Checkmate agent has been named after the best-regarded catalog of the Italian agent Gioachino Greco. It is finished with the aid of the use of the bishop to govern the black king, the use of the black infantry after which through the queen, to check at the king, transferring him to the aspect of the chessboard.

The Wife in File H

H-report mate is a way to test. The inspector includes using an alley that attacks the black king, that's supported via the bishop. This frequently takes place after the castles of the black king inside the position of maids in his kingdom. White normally enters this position after a chain of sacrifices in case h.

Pair Rook

The pair of rooks consists of a white rook, knight, and infantry in conjunction with a black infantry to limit the escape of the black king. The knight protects the rook, and the infantry protects the knight.

The Assignment of the King and The 2 Bishops

The king's venture and the 2 bishops are one of four essential functions alongside the queen's wife, Matt's container, and the bishop and knight. It happens that the king, with bishops, forces the bare king at the nook of the image to pressure a likely wife.

The King and the 2 Knights Have a Project

In a sport of two knights, the king and the 2 knights cannot force an empty king to be arrested. If the empty king is gambling correctly, this last sport has to be drawn. A player makes a mistake most effective if the participant with the empty king is wrong or has already been inside the corner of the board.

Lolly's Neighbor

Lolli's wife is a fashionable manner to check. The summary consists of the infiltration of Black's fiancé's position using his leg and queen.

The queen normally arrives in rectangular h6, the usage of the sacrifices in report h, dubbed after Giambattista Lolli.

A Colleague of Max Lange

Max Lange's spouse is a general manner to test. The Czech officer is appointed Max Lange. It is done by the use of the bishop and queen to manipulate the king.

Murphy's Mate

Murphy's spouse is a well-known manner to check. Named after Paul Murphy, this is achieved by the use of a bishop to assault the black king and a rook and a black and white pedestrian to fasten him up. In many ways, he's very much like Corner's wife.

Opera Colleague

Mate Opera is a widespread manner to check. It works through attacking the king within the returned with a rook using a bishop to protect him. A pedestal or other piece apart from the Knight of the Enemy King is used to restrict his movement.

This teammate became named the Opera after the interpretation of Paul Morphy in 1858 in a Paris opera against Dunk Carl de Brunswick and Count Isouard.

Comrade Pillsbury

Pillsbury's wife is a preferred verifier, named after Harry Nelson Pillsbury. As shown at the right, it works with the aid of attacking the king or a pier or bishop. The king can be in g8 or h8 during checkmate.

The Spouse of the Queen

The queen is one of 4 vital missions along with Boxing, King and two Bishops, and Ismail and Knight.

It happens when the party with the queen and king forces the naked queen to the brink or corner of the council. The queen completely examines the naked king, and the pleasant king supports her.

Reti's Mate

Reti marriage is a popular way to test. The Czech officer is known as Richard Reti. Do this via grabbing the enemy king with four portions which are inside the flying fields after which attacking him with a bishop who's covered by a rook or a queen.

Colleague Mate

Intimate pairing is a well-known way to test. It occurs that a knight controls the kingdom, which is suppressed (besieged) by its thick portions, and he has nowhere to move, and there is virtually no manner to overcome the knight.

The Neighbor's Sleep

Suffocation is a trendy way of checking. It is performed the usage of the knights to assault the rival king and the bishop to restrict the king's getaway routes.

Swallow's Tail

Swallow's tail, also referred to as Guéridon's wife is a standard manner to check. It works via attacking the enemy king with a queen included using a rook. The rooks of the enemy king block his escape device. He is very just like Epaulette's spouse.

Chapter 10: Simple Advice On Thinking And Acting

The chess game ends when you check the opponent's king, or his opponent resigns. However, as long as this does not happen, the other party struggles to prevent it. The more you win, the more frustrating the fight.

Likewise, don't move except if you need to. The beat is one of the most significant components of chess: it figures out who moves. It might choose your destiny (or your opponent's) that your play will be passed the point of no return. The most ideal approach to stay aware of yourself is to ensure that each move improves your system. Also, any movement that threatens your opponent should force him to respond. Otherwise, if your opponent does not feel pressure, it is just more time to think about how to hurt yourself.

Chess is about learning the prediction, seeing the future, and planning. Before doing so, a plan is good if it seems successful. As the idea progresses, a player draws empty squares that he can control later in the game. Choosing the best parts for maneuver is like life; you have the most use for the materials available. Everything plans the advancement of a single objective or objective.

Tips on the Best Way to Play Chess Better

Chess has been around for a long time. This is a game that has occurred in families for quite a long time, played in parks far and wide, and even incites the brains of detainees in jails. After a long game and your mind is worn out, numerous individuals' figure, "How might I play better chess?"

The sequences that good players use to win games may seem complicated. But most are based on a few general concepts that are intelligently and continuously combined.

Here are three hints you can add to your chess stockpile to assist you with understanding the specialty of winning chess.

1. Twofold Danger

One of the essential thoughts in chess is a twofold risk. When all is said in done, a twofold danger is any move you make, which presents two issues to the next gathering at the same time.

Since each player can only make one move at a time, your opponent has only one chance to eliminate one of the threats.

Next time you run another one. Maybe your first move is to check your king and attack another piece simultaneously, or maybe you threaten one of his pieces and threaten to inspect elsewhere. The result is the same: your opponent must make the next move to counter your threat against his king, and then he must take the other piece you threatened.

2. The Weak Piece

Another significant idea in chess is a free piece. A loose piece is simply a piece that has no protection. It is common for players to leave unauthorized tracks here and there. They look safe enough until they are attacked. But the pieces released set perfect goals for the double threat described at the moment.

Suppose your queen makes a fork while attacking her opponent's king and one of his rooks. He moves his king. Now you can use the queen to protect your face - if not protected. But if this rook is protected, you can't use it, because it will cost a lot: your queen will be captured later.

We can turn this into a practical game recommendation. You always want to be aware of the free parts on the board. Any piece that your opponent does not protect is a possible target for a tactical attack. Any piece that is not protected is vulnerable. You want to not only observe the free parts of the enemy but also to look for ways to create them.

3. Constraints

Therefore, convulsions and threats of the husband are considered obligatory. In other words, these are the moves that make your opponent choose from a set of possible answers. They are the essence of tactical chess. These allow you to dictate your opponent's movements and thus control how the board thinks you will look two or three or more steps today.

Here and there in chess, you move however you'd like to, and afterward, the rival does anything he desires. Other times: If, for example, a knight captures him with his bishop, he is about to have to take your bishop back. Otherwise, he is a short piece and will probably lose. (Other parts on both sides are gradually changed, and you will end up with only the remaining portion that attacks the board.)

Chapter 11:   Essential Tactics For Beginners

In this chapter, we will be discussing the various "tactics" you can employ to help you gain more points than your opponent, defend your pieces, and ultimately win each game. Without further ado, let's get started.

Here are some of the tactics we will be talking about:

- Forks

- Pins

- Attacking a defender

- Skewers

- Discovered attacks

- Eliminating a defender

- Double checks

- Discovered checks

- Trapping pieces, etc.

Looking at the names of some of the tactics, you would think they are complex – however, that's not true. Most of the tactics are simple and straightforward moves which you can master through constant practice.

Among the tactics listed above, the ones that are often used the most by players are forks, pins, skewers. We shall talk about them first before giving attention to others.

The Fork

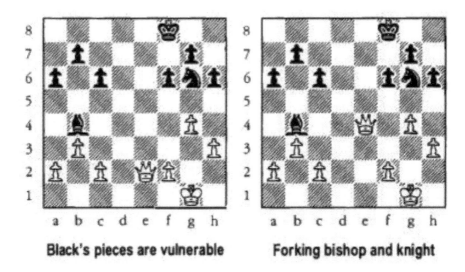

Black's pieces are vulnerable   Forking bishop and knight

The fork is one of the easiest tactics you can use to gain some material advantage over your opponent. How does a fork occur? Picture how a garden fork, for instance, looks in real life. A fork has one handle and several tongues. In chess, a fork occurs when you use a single piece to attack two or more pieces belonging to your enemy at the same time.

In the first diagram shown above, you can see that many black pieces are vulnerable to attacks. If White moves his queen from e3 to e4 as seen in the second diagram, the white queen on e4 will be attacking the black knight on g6 and the bishop on b4. Look at the second diagram for clarification.

The two black pieces that are being attacked do not have any defense, as you can see – so black will definitely lose one of them. When two pieces are forked, this can also be referred to as a "double attack."

Forking with Check

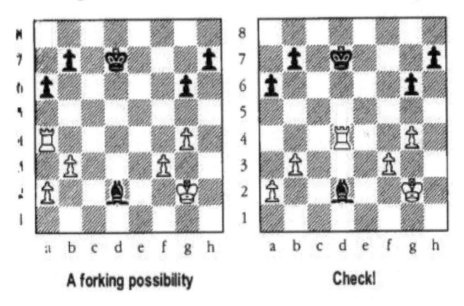

A forking possibility   Check!

In the first diagram above, the black and bishop on the d-file are open to attacks at the same time – the white rook on a4 can fork the two of them. If White moves his rook from a4 to d4, an important move, Black will be left in a tight corner, as seen in the second diagram.

In the second diagram, Black has no choice but to move his king out of check. White will make a second move by playing 2 Rxd2, thus gaining three points.

Fork with Other Pieces

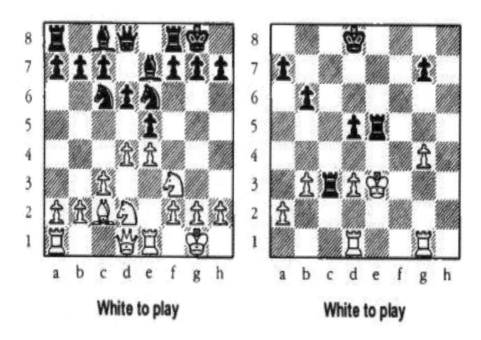

White to play   White to play

Fork, unlike most other chess tactics, can be performed using any chess piece of choice. In the first diagram above, it is White's turn to play – if he plays 1 d5! then he would be using a pawn to fork two black knights. Black will only be able to move one of the knights, leaving the other at the mercy of the white pawn.

In the second diagram, the black rook on e5 is checking the white king on e3 – White has to move his king out of check. If White plays 1 Kd4, he will successfully fork the two black rooks. In this case, Black must move one of the rooks as there is no way other of protecting the two of them.

The Family Fork

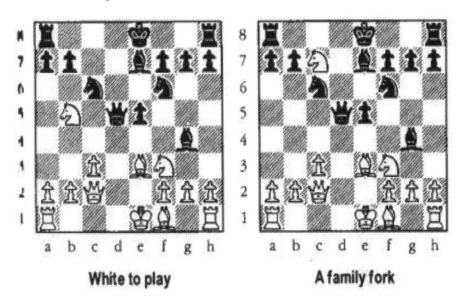

White to play   A family fork

You already know that a fork occurs when a piece attacks two opposing pieces at once. Well, a family fork occurs when a piece attacks more than two enemy pieces at once. While any piece on the board can carry out a fork, the knight is well known for performing family forks.

In the diagram shown above, it is White's turn to play – if he moves his knight from b5 to c7, that will be a family fork because, in that location, the white knight can attack the black queen on d5, the black king on e8 and the black rook on a8. Look at the second diagram for clarification.

If Black plays 1... Kd7, i.e., moving his king from e8 to d7, White will capture the next black piece of importance, which is the queen on d5. If for his second move, White plays 2 Nxd5 and Black plays 2... Nxd5, at the end of the transactions, White will gain a queen for a knight, which is six points.

That's it for forks, let's proceed to talk about pins.

Pins

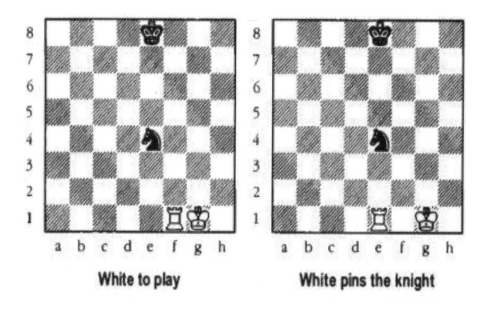

White to play   **White pins the knight**

While fork is a powerful tactic, pin remains one of the most powerful tactics or weapons you can use to win a point or deliver checkmate in chess. How does a pin occur?

If you attack two enemy pieces that cannot move beyond the line of attack without making a more valuable piece behind them vulnerable, then you have performed a pin. In other words, it is a way of pinning two opposing pieces to a line of attack because if they move, they will be exposing a more valuable piece to a threat.

Pins are of two types: normal pins and pins against kings.

In a typical pin against the king, a pinned piece cannot move, else it will expose his king. Pin against the king is the more powerful of the two types of pins. In the first diagram shown above, the black king behind the knight on the same file is vulnerable. In the second diagram, the white rook pins the black knight. If the black knight moves, he will be exposing his king, and that's illegal.

Attacking the Pinned Piece

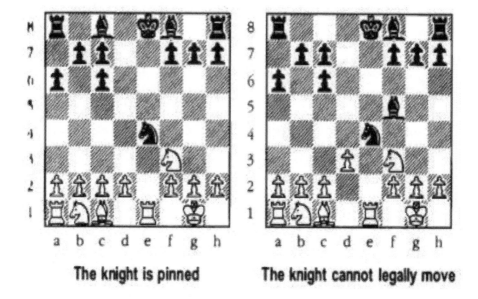

The knight is pinned   The knight cannot legally move

Your main aim of pinning an enemy piece is to allow you to protect your own pieces. In the first diagram shown above, White has pinned the black knight on e4 to the black king on e8. So, Black cannot legally move the e4-knight.

If Black protects his e4 knight by playing 1... Bf5, White will display his power by moving his d-pawn from d2 to d3; hence, attacking the black knight on e4 yet again. On the next move, White will play 3 dxe4, capturing Black's knight on e4.

Pinning a Major Piece Against a King

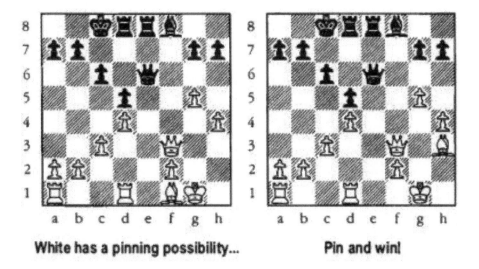

White has a pinning possibility...   Pin and win!

In the previous example, we looked at the possibility of pinning a knight against a king – but even more powerful pieces can still be pinned against a king. For instance, you can pin a rook or a queen against a king.

In the first diagram above, you can easily see that White has a pinning possibility – the black queen and king are occupying the same diagonal, which gives White a pinning chance.

If White plays 1 Bh3 (see the second diagram for clarification), he will successfully pin the black queen against the king, thus granting White a lot of material advantages. In that pinned position, the Black's queen can move, but only along that diagonal, which means that the pinning took away most of the black queen's powers.

In a follow-up move, White will play Bxe6, gaining six points.

A pinned Piece Doesn't Have Much Power!

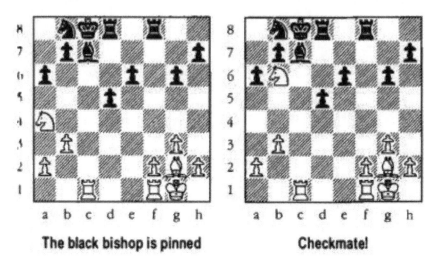

The black bishop is pinned   **Checkmate!**

This is commonsense – if a piece is pinned, the piece loses a lot of power.

Let's examine the first diagram above – the white rook on c1 is comfortably pinning the black bishop on c7 against the black king on c8. Interestingly, the king protects the black bishop, meaning that the white rook on c1 cannot favorably capture it.

Nevertheless, White can still make other powerful moves and gain leverage while the other black pieces are still pinned. If White plays 1 Nb6 mate, then that's checkmate and game over for Black. See the second diagram for clarification. In the second diagram, you can see that there is no escape route for the black king after White moved his knight from a4 to b6.

Normal Pins

Here, we want to consider the second type of pins – normal pins.

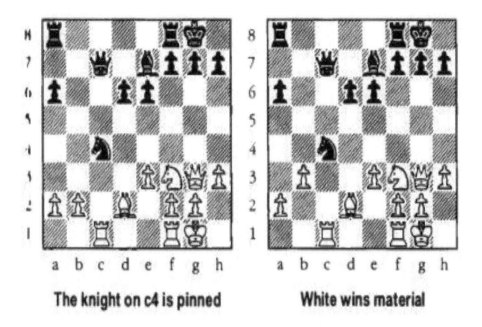

The knight on c4 is pinned   **White wins material**

Unlike a "pin against a king" that is often more vicious, a normal pin, just as the name implies, is less vicious, although it can still be leveraged to cause serious damage to the other team.

Look at the diagram above, for instance, White's rook on c1 is comfortably pinning the black knight on c4 against the back queen on c7. Even though Black can legally move the knight on c4; that would entail exposing the powerful black queen on c7 to attack.

At the moment, the knight on c4 is protecting the queen along the c-file, so if White plays 1 Rxc4; that would be a terrible move because Black will retaliate by playing 1... Qxc4.

If White should play 1 b3; then that's an excellent move because Black must lose the knight by playing 1... Nxd2. Then White would play 2 Rxc7, leaving Black to play 2... Nxf1. For his third move, White will play 3 Kxf1. At the end of the transaction, Black will lose some points (I will leave you to figure out the number of points Black lose in that transaction).

A PINNED PIECE DOESN'T PROTECT

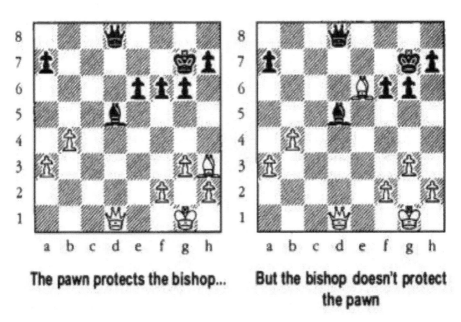

The pawn protects the bishop...   But the bishop doesn't protect the pawn

When a piece is pinned, it loses a lot of its power − this is something that anybody should know. In the first diagram shown above, you can see that the white queen on d1 is pinning the black bishop on d5 against the black queen on d8. You have to also notice that a white bishop on h3 is attacking a black pawn on e6.

Now, it is quite interesting to see that the black pawn on e6 can actively protect the black bishop on d5. However, the black bishop on d5 cannot protect the black pawn on e6. The reason is simple, the black bishop on d5 is being pinned, and any move to protect the black pawn on e6 will see Black losing his queen. In the above scenario, there is no escape for Black; he must lose material.

The Skewer

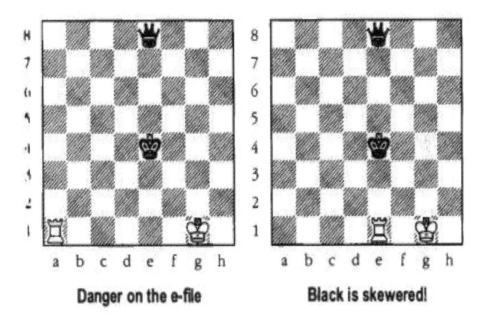

Danger on the e-file   Black is skewered!

A skewer and a pin have almost the same characteristics.

When you attack an enemy piece such that the attacked piece cannot escape without exposing another enemy piece of equal, higher, or near-equal value to attack, then you have carried out a skewer.

Look at the diagram above, Black is liable to be skewed as you can see. If White plays 1 Re1+, it means that White will be skewing the black king on e4 to the black queen on e8.

In this situation, Black cannot move his queen; he must get his king out of check first, thus exposing his queen to attack. So, in this case, the black king must move, making way for the white rook on e1 (as seen in the second diagram) to capture the black queen on e8.

Skewering

White has a skewer opportunity

Just like pinning a piece, if you want to skewer an opponent's piece successfully, you will need to do it with those pieces of yours that can cover long ranges on the board. Examples of such long-range pieces include bishops, rooks, and queens. This is quite unlike forks that can be performed using any piece at all.

In the diagram shown above, for instance, White can play 1 Rc1, which is quite straightforward. If that happens, that means Black's bishop on c4 will get skewered to the black knight on c5 by White's rook. As can be seen on the diagram, Black's bishop will have no escape route except to subject the black knight to attack. If the black bishop moves to a6-square, for instance, White will attack the black knight on c5 using the rook on c1. So, either way, Black must lose a piece.

Attacking a Skewered Piece

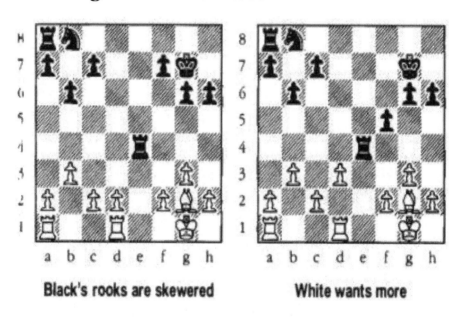

Black's rooks are skewered White wants more

In the first diagram shown above, Black's two rooks are skewered. At least one of the rooks must be captured by the white bishop on g2. Now, if the black rook on e4 moves to the d4-square, for instance, the white bishop on g2 will still capture the second black rook on a8.

In this situation, Black can make a desperate attempt to cut his losses by playing 1... f5. With Black's pawn now on f5, it means the black rook on e4 is now protected. If for the second move, White plays 2 Bxe4, and Black plays 2... fxe4, it then means that White gained two points from the transaction.

But if for his second move, White plays 2 d3, as can be seen in the second diagram, it then means that White has prepared the way to capture the black rook on e4 with a pawn (a low-valued piece). If that happens, White will win more material.

Attacking a Defender

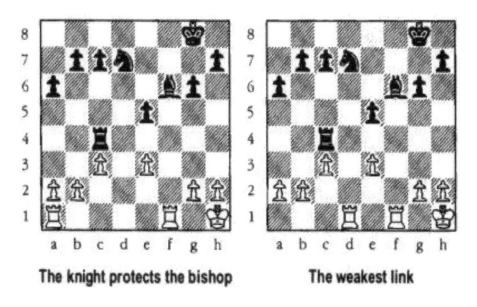

The knight protects the bishop   The weakest link

Attacking a defender is another chess tactic that you can use to win some points and ultimately deliver a checkmate to your opponent's king. What does it mean to attack a defender?

Let's assume that one of your pieces is already threatening an opponent's piece, if the threatened piece is being defended or protected by another; you can use one of your free pieces to attack the defender. This will most likely collapse your opponent's defense. Once this happens, you can move in for the kill.

So, to perform this tactic, you have to attack an enemy piece. Then proceed to attack the defender of the enemy piece. In the first diagram shown above, White's rook on f1 is already threatening the black bishop on f6. Black's bishop is not totally alone as he is defended or protected by the black knight on d7.

Now, if White wants to perform an "attack the defender" tactic, he would have to attack the defending black knight. So, if White plays 1 Rad1, he gains a lot of advantages. This single move by White will weaken Black's defenses. If Black should leave his knight on d7, White will use his rook on d1 to capture it. If Black also decides to move his rook from d7, White will capture the black bishop on f6. So, no matter the move made by Black, White will gain a piece or some points. See the second diagram above for clarification.

Eliminating a Defender

This tactic is similar to the one we just discussed. But in this case, rather than attacking the defender, you eliminate the defending piece entirely.

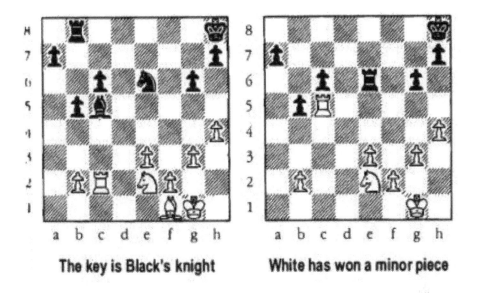

The key is Black's knight   **White has won a minor piece**

There are instances when you cannot simply attack a defender, probably because there is another piece that will still defend the attacked. So, in such an instance, what you do is to eliminate the defender entirely. Eliminating the defender is sometimes called destroying the guard.

In the first diagram shown above, the white rook on c2 is attacking the black bishop on c5. However, there is a black knight on d6 that is actively defending the black bishop on c5. Now, if White wants to attack the defender, which in this case is the black knight, White would have to play 1 Bh3.

Even with the above move by White, Black can still attempt to protect his knight by playing 1... Re8. However, this move alone will be enough to protect Black's threatened pieces entirely because, for his second move, White will still eliminate the black knight on e6.

Black will make a second move and play 2... Rxe6. For his third move, White can easily play 3 Rxc5, thus making him gain 3 points net (I will leave you to figure this out yourself). See the second diagram for clarification.

The Discovered Attack

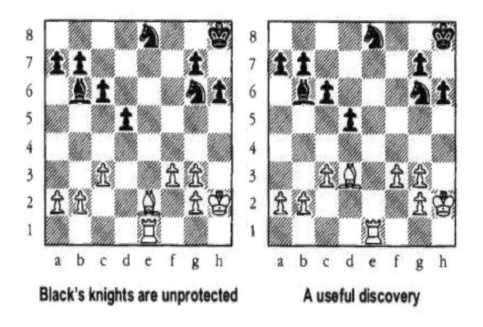

Black's knights are unprotected   A useful discovery

In addition to the other chess tactics that we have discussed in this chapter; the discovered attack is yet another powerful tactic you can use to gain some quick points occasionally.

In the first diagram shown above, you can see that the White bishop and the white rook are on the same e-file. If the bishop moves to another file, rank, or diagonal, that movement will expose the black knight on e8 to an attack from the white rook on e1.

What makes the example in the first diagram above more interesting is that if the white bishop moves to d3, for instance, he will yet again attack the black knight on g6. So, in this case, Black is under double attack. See the second diagram for clarification. So, no matter the move that Black makes, he will definitely lose one of his knights.

Uncovering an Attack by Capturing

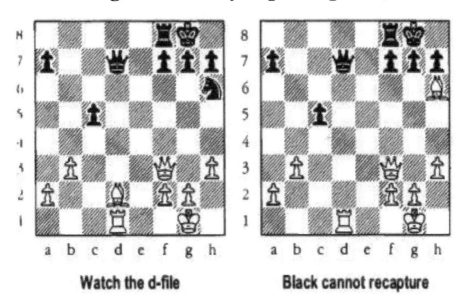

Watch the d-file   Black cannot recapture

In the previous example, you saw how to uncover an attack by moving a piece and exposing another that is behind. In this particular example, you will learn how to uncover an attack by capturing another enemy piece.

In the first diagram shown above, the white rook and the black queen are on the same file. This sends a warning sign to White, but White can flip the situation to his advantage by uncovering an attack.

White will need to play 1 Bxh6 – this is an excellent move because Black will not want to use his pawn on g7 to recapture the white bishop on h6. Rather, at this point, black will be more interested in saving his queen. Also, notice that Black cannot use his queen to capture the white rook on d1 because the white queen on f3 is actively protecting the rook. This is one of the things that makes this particular uncovering an attack by capturing tactic work effectively.

Uncovering an Attack with Check

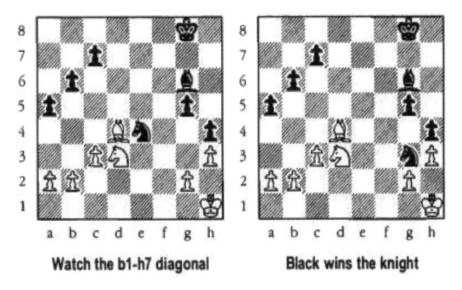

Watch the b1-h7 diagonal   **Black wins the knight**

This is another variation of the discovered attack tactic. This happens when the piece that moved in order to uncover an attack also delivers a check to the enemy's king at the same time. Just like you would imagine, this variation of the tactic is more powerful than the other two we have discussed. The reason for that shouldn't be hard for you to guess. When the piece that moved to uncover an attack delivers a check, the opponent will be more interested in protecting his king and moving him out of check.

In the first diagram shown above, if Black plays, 1... Ng3+, then he has not only delivered a check to the white king on h1, but he has also uncovered an attack on the white knight on d3. In the second diagram, you can see that the black bishop on g6 is comfortably attacking the white knight on d3.

White has no option here than to move his king away from check. If White moves his king from h1 to h2, Black will capture the white knight on d3 using the black bishop on g6.

In the first diagram, notice that if Black had uncovered an attack by moving his knight on e4 to f2 instead of g3, Black would have been the one to lose his knight (I need you to figure this out yourself).

Discovered Checks

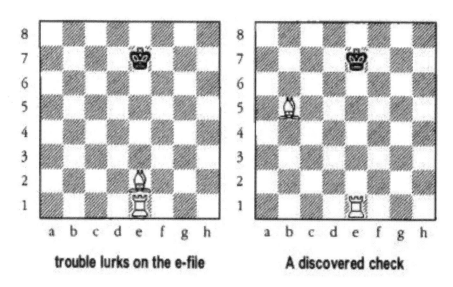

trouble lurks on the e-file   A discovered check

A discovered check has almost everything in common with the discovered attack tactic we discussed in the preceding section.

152

However, discovered check delivers more deadly blows to the opponent that discovered attacks. So, how does it occur?

If an enemy's king occupies the same rank, file, or diagonal with two of your own pieces, you can perform a discovered check by moving one of your pieces away from the diagonal, rank, or file such that the other of your pieces behind would deliver a check to your opponent's king.

In the first diagram shown above, both the white rook, bishop, and black king are occupying the same e-file. As you can see in the diagram, trouble looms for Black. If White moves his bishop from e2 to b5, for instance, as can be seen in the second diagram, then White has discovered check. Black will have to put in some effort to move his king away from check.

Damaging Discovered Checks

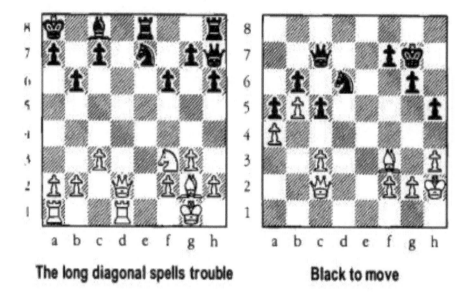

The long diagonal spells trouble   **Black to move**

If an opponent uses the discovered attack or check tactic against you – you can flip the situation around and still stand at an advantage. How's that possible? Look at the diagrams above.

In the first diagram, if White plays 1 Ng5+, it wouldn't matter that in the knight's new position, which is the g5-square, Black's pawns are threatening the white knight. What's more important is that White has uncovered a check on the black king on a8 (uncovered attack: notice the white bishop on g2 attacking the king). Black will have to move his king to b8 or use any of his other pieces to block the line of fire.

Whatever moves he makes, White will make a second move and use his knight on g5 to capture the black queen on h7.

Double Checks

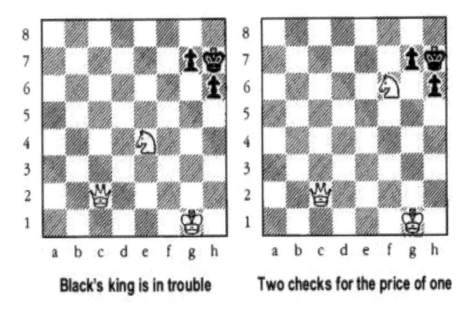

Black's king is in trouble   **Two checks for the price of one**

In the first diagram shown above, you can see that the black king on h7 is in deep trouble because if White moves his knight from e4 to f6, the black king will be facing double checks.

Double checks, like a chess weapon, have more power than discovered attacks or checks. As you would imagine, it would be hard for the king that is being double-checked to move out of check. By definition, a double check occurs when a piece moves off a line, rank, or diagonal to deliver a check to a king while still uncovering another piece that delivers a second check to the already checked king. To understand how the tactics work or how it is performed, look at the diagrams shown above.

We already explained that if White moves his knight from e4 to f6, the knight will deliver a check to the black king. Not only that, the movement of the knight will uncover the White queen on c2 that will also deliver a check to the black king.

As you can see in the second diagram, the black king will have to move away from check by moving to h8, as that's the only square still available to him. After Black moves his king to h8, White can easily deliver a checkmate by moving his queen from c2 to either h7 or c8

Double-Check Leading to Mate

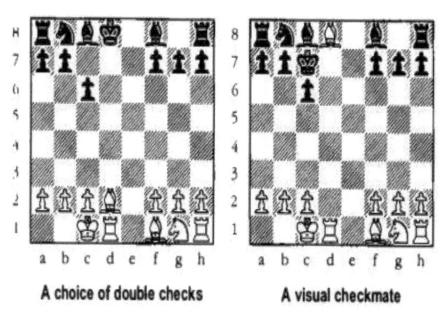

A choice of double checks   A visual checkmate

A double-check is one of those situations you don't want to face as a chess beginner, but it can be so pleasant when you use it against an opponent.

What makes double-check unpleasant is that your king is being checked by two enemy pieces. Your only option would be to move the king. You cannot block the line of fire since there are two pieces that are checking your king. Also, you cannot use another piece to capture the checking piece because there are two of them, and you are allowed to make one move at a time.

In the first diagram shown above, White has the chance to perform the double-check tactic on Black. If White plays 1 Bg5+ or 1 Ba5+, he will deliver double checks to the black king on d8. Playing 1 Bg5+ will be more beneficial to White as he checkmates the black king on his second move.

If Black plays 1... Kc7, White makes a second move by playing 2 Bc7 mate, thus ending the game. Look at the second diagram for clarification.

Checkmating Threats to Win Material

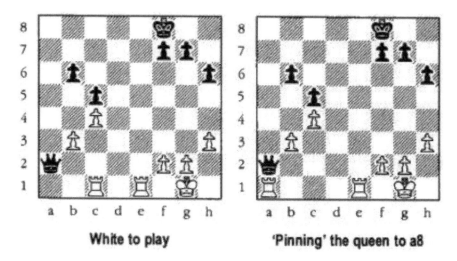

White to play

'Pinning' the queen to a8

Many times, when playing chess, you can use the threat of a potential checkmate to gain some advantage and force your opponent to make some moves that will benefit you.

In the first diagram shown above, it is White's turn to play – and he can easily play 1 Ra1, a powerful move that will see him attacking the black queen a2. The black queen will have to be constrained to that square and allow White to attack it because if the black queen moves, White will use one of his rooks to deliver a checkmate.

If Black plays 1... Qd2; that would be like postponing the evil day because White will play 2 Ra8+. So, in this situation, the only choice that Black has would be to forfeit his queen for White's rook by playing 1... Qxa1, leaving White to play 2 Rxa1. See the second diagram for clarification.

Example 2 on How to Use Checkmating Threats to Win Material

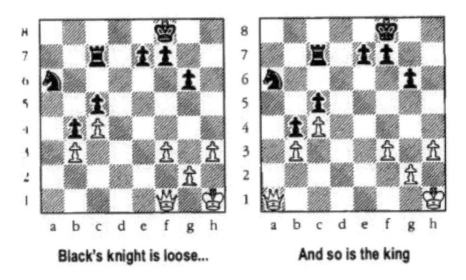

| Black's knight is loose... | And so is the king |

If you look closely at the first diagram above, you will see that the black knight on a6 is loose and unguarded. White can leverage that to win material. You should also notice that the black king is highly vulnerable in his current state.

If White plays 1 Qa1, then the new position of the white queen will be threatening the black knight on a6 and the black king on f8 (by playing Qh8 mate). Black must do something to protect his king from the impending checkmate, so he will be left with no other option than to sacrifice his knight.

Remember, what the White queen is doing in the second diagram is a proper way of forking. The white queen is forking both the black knight and the black king.

Trapping Pieces

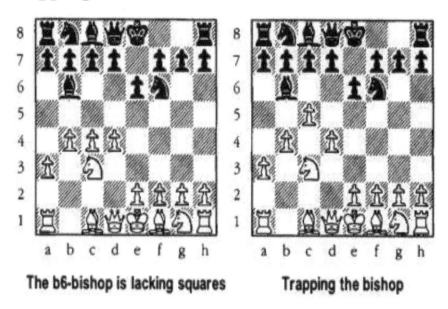

The b6-bishop is lacking squares   Trapping the bishop

This is yet another important tactic that you can use to gain material. You can perform trapping of pieces by using a group of pawns to guide your own pieces and delivering attacks.

In the first diagram shown above, Black in an earlier move had the opportunity to exchange his bishop for the white knight on c3, but he didn't utilize it. Now, White is going to teach him a bitter lesson. It is the turn of White to play.

White plays 1 c5. Black cannot use his bishop to capture the white pawn on c5, and as there is another white pawn on d4 protecting it. The other box, the a5-square available to the black bishop, is also being protected by the white pawn on b4. In this situation, Black's only option would be to lose his bishop to a pawn, which is a net loss of 2 points, if we want to talk in terms of material gains or loss.

Trapping the Queen

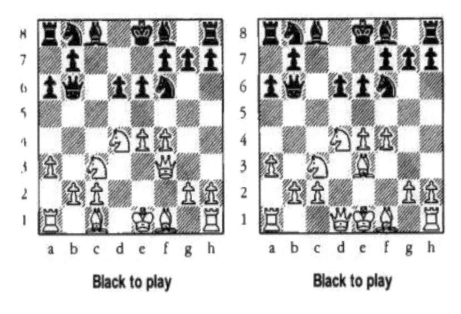

Black to play   Black to play

One common mistake that most chess beginners make is that they often develop their queens prematurely. If you do that, you will be exposing one of your most powerful pieces to an attack. If your opponent knows what they are doing, they can easily trap the queen, and you will lose many points.

In the first diagram shown above, it is the turn of Black to play after White had made a previous move. Black plays 1... Qxd4. This is a wrong move, as you will soon find out. White will make a second move and play 2 Be3. If White successfully traps Black's queen in the middle of the board, then Black must give up the queen.

In the second diagram, a similar scenario can easily play out. Again, it is the turn of Black to play after White had made an initial move. Black plays 1... Qxb2. White will simply play 2 Na4; thus trapping the black queen mid-board.

Deflection

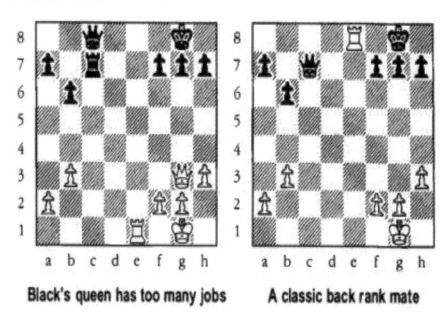

Black's queen has too many jobs   A classic back rank mate

Just as the name implies, deflection is a tactic used to lure an enemy piece to stay away from the job of defending a particular square or line.

In the first diagram shown, it is the job of the black queen to ensure that the black king on g8 and the black rook on c7 are duly protected. Black's queen needs to ensure that White doesn't move his rook from e1 to e8, as that would be a typical back rank mate.

Since the black queen seems to have a lot of jobs to do, the queen can be said to be "overloaded." White will leverage this weakness to play 1 Qxc7. This is purely a deflection move by White. Black will have no other option than to play 1... Qxc7.

If Black doesn't play 1... Qxc7, he will lose a rook and still lose another piece. White will complete the move by playing 2 Re8 mate. The game is over for Black.

Another Example of Deflection

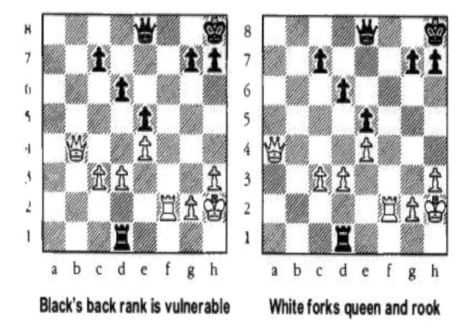

Black's back rank is vulnerable   White forks queen and rook

This is another example of deflection but one that is a bit complex than the previous one we saw.

In the first diagram, Black's back rank is porous, and White can capitalize on that to make a material gain. If White plays 1 Qa4; that singular move will attempt to deflect the black queen and take the queen's attention away from the f8-square.

Playing 1 Qa4 by White will not only deflect the attention of the black queen away from f8-square, but the white queen will also be forking the black rook and queen at the same time.

If Black plays 1... Qxa4, White will simply play 2 Rf8 mate. But if the black queen moves up the a-file, then the white queen will capture the black rook on d1. No matter the move that Black makes, White's second move must end up delivering a checkmate to the black king.

Chapter 12:   Errors to Avoid

Carelessness can bring undesirable results. This is the same with chess. Some players don't lose because they lack the skill. Rather, they are not very careful with their moves and end up doing something disadvantageous for them. This can eventually cost them the game.

Here are the three common accidents in chess that every chess player should be aware of. Knowing these will allow them to spot possible scenarios that will lead to it and eventually avoid it.

Losing Your Piece for Nothing

Capturing one of your opponent's pieces (or having one of yours captured) is a normal part of the game. It is common for players to bait their opponent to capture one of their pieces because another piece is guarding that square in case it is captured. If you should lose a piece, the opponent should also lose one of theirs. However, it can be costly for a player to lose any piece but don't get anything in return. This situation can be treated as if they gave something to the opponent for free.

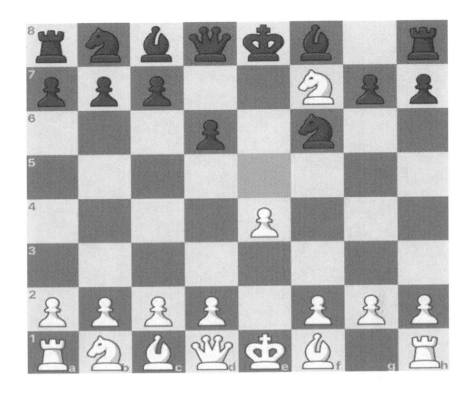

Here is an example:

In the image above, it can be seen that White moved his knight to f7 and threaten Black's queen and rook. However, what White fails to notice is that the square where it landed is guarded by Black's king. Since the knight is not guarded by any other piece in case of capture, Black can capture the knight for free!

Sometimes, hanging pieces are not that obvious. The image below appears like a normal opening sequence for the game.

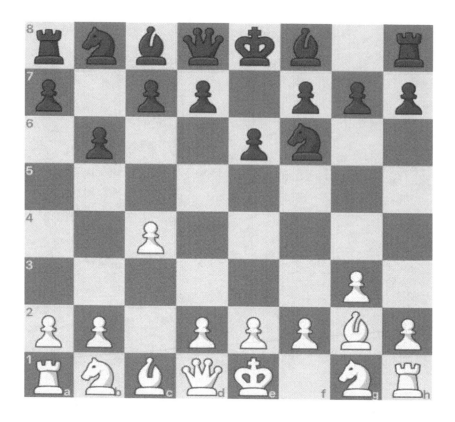

However, if one is to look closely, White can capture Black's rook on the other corner of the board. Free 5 points for White! Even if Black decides to block the bishop, it will surely be able to capture another piece before getting captured.

A player should look at all areas carefully so that having a "hanging" piece can be avoided. Obviously, this is a mistake that you want your enemies to commit, as it can give you an advantage.

Losing a Piece with Higher Value

It was mentioned earlier that having one of your pieces captured for free is bad. This opens the idea that you should at least get something in exchange for that piece. However, this doesn't mean that we should settle for pieces that have a lower value. Capturing an opponent's piece with a lower value than ours is not good either.

If the game drags on and this trend of getting an "uneven trade" continues, the player whose higher value pieces are traded for lower value ones will end up with a deficit and eventually lose the game because their power is significantly reduced.

169

The image above shows that White took out his queen way too early. Black responded by moving his pawn to d5 and opening the bishop for capture. If White decides to take on the bait, his queen will be easily captured even if Black's bishop has been sacrificed. By simply referring back to the point value of pieces, it can be seen that White will lose 9 points while Black will only lose 3.

Players should remember that even though capturing multiple pieces can help them get an advantage, being able to target and capture high-value pieces is still better. Trades should be based on the value of the piece, not on how many can be captured in exchange for a high-value piece. Even if you are able to capture three pawns, it would still be an uneven trade if your queen or rook gets captured because of those small pieces.

Your Pieces Are Outnumbered

It is common for a player to offer one of his pieces as bait so that he can capture anything that attempts to capture that piece, especially if a piece with a higher value will be involved. However, there are times when a piece is not guarded enough. If the opponent sees an area that does not have enough protection, he will surely exploit that weakness. He may even be willing to sacrifice some of his lower value pieces just so he can capture your higher value pieces. In this case, it's important to defend possible weak areas more. By doing this, your opponent will hesitate in capturing one of your pieces.

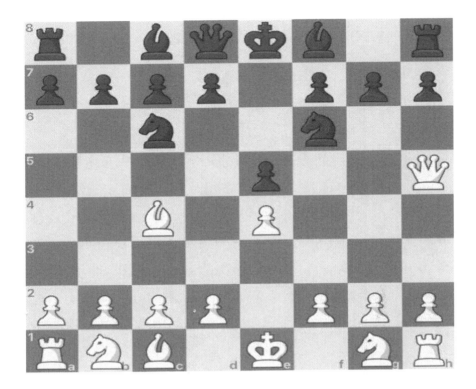

The image above is an example of the four-move tactic that can win games for White. This tactic exploits the weakness of the pawn in f7. With White to move, it can be seen that the said pawn is only protected by Black's King. However, that same piece is threatened by White's bishop and queen. Since the defense for that area is not sufficient, White can capture that area without any problems, get protected by the bishop, and checkmate the opponent.

Chapter 13: Apply What You Have Learned and Solve the Various Puzzles

If you want to systematically improve your chess skills and become a Grandmaster, you will require a work plan. This sounds much easier than it actually is. Players have different preferences: some like openings, some prefer to solve tactics, while some just like to play. However, in order to achieve overall progress, you must work systematically on all stages of the game. Think of it as reading seven different books at the same time instead of reading just one.

Once you decide to create a work plan, you are already one step further on your improvement journey. At this stage, you should consider getting a coach. If you already have one, great. If you don't, try to get a good one. Be aware that price is not a guarantee of quality. Generally, higher titled players make better coaches. They have a deeper understanding of the game and can make chess principles easier to understand. There are exceptions of course, but as a general rule: A Grandmaster knows much more than a Master. Discuss your work plan with your coach and let him help you create it. If you don't have the means to afford a coach or you simply don't want one, you'll have to create a plan yourself. I will now give you some pointers.

The first question to ask yourself is: how much time will you invest in chess? It's imperative you divide that time amongst all different segments of the game.

Openings

Working on openings does not necessarily mean checking all games played and memorizing all the moves. It does not mean you should read an openings book and extract everything from there either. There is much more to it.

First of all, the situation depends on whether or not you already have an opening repertoire. If you have one, you should want to improve it by adding some of your own analysis or widen it by adding some sidelines. Be sure to constantly check for new games played in your lines. Search for new ideas using your brain as well as your chess engine. Even if you don't find anything useful, you will become familiar with this opening and you will improve your understanding of it. You must not neglect your openings and have to update your opening base frequently.

If you still don't have an opening repertoire, you have to start by adding nicely coordinated openings. You should realize, you have to cover all possible opening choices of your opponents. If you are about to add an opening to your repertoire, you must first check all the recent games played by strong players using this opening. Concentrate on the middlegame structures which arise from its use. Ask yourself if these positions suit you and whether or not you want to play them. If the answer is affirmative, then work on finding the main lines. The best advice I can give is to closely check the latest games played by Grandmasters. It's almost certain they were well prepared in the specific lines and are up to date with current line developments. After you have done so, keep your lines updated and keep searching for improvements.

Middlegames

Studying middlegames is very closely connected to studying openings. From your openings, some typical middlegame pawn structures, i.e. isolated pawn, hanging pawns, blocked center – will arise. Arm yourself with books or videos of Grandmasters explaining these structures. The authors of this eBook will be more than happy to recommend appropriate literature. Ask questions and communicate with titled players. Nowadays, you have plenty of opportunities to chat with chess Grandmasters - whether it's on Twitch or your favorite chess app. Perhaps you have some Grandmasters visiting your favorite chess club? Try to come up with concrete questions to ask them. Try not to be too aggressive, but don't get discouraged if you don't get your answers immediately.

Pay attention to open and closed positions, opposite side castles, and positions with a pair of bishops. Similar to openings, you can search for new ideas in middlegames as well. You should arm yourself with the knowledge of recognizing your positional weaknesses and strengths as well as that of your opponent's. Try to understand good and bad pieces, where they need to be, and whether or not they need to be exchanged. By learning these things, you will set a foundation for middlegame strategic planning.

Endings

When studying endings, you must start from the basics. First, you have to study easier theoretical endings with fewer pieces and slowly advance to more complex ones. If you study endings from Keres or Fine, they will give you a very good base and teach you all the important principles that you should know. Advanced endgame techniques are simply implementation of all those principles accompanied by decent calculations.

Calculation Technique

To improve your calculation technique, you must organize the concept in a systematic manner. It is easy for me to guess how a beginner or even an intermediate player calculates his moves. He begins by looking at the first move. He sees something he doesn't like, then jumps immediately to a second move. In the middle of his calculation, he notices a third option, looks at it for a minute, then reverts back to the first move. He then notices a fourth option... and so on and so forth. Do you recognize yourself in this situation? Don't worry, we've all been there.

What you must get into the habit of doing first is establishing move candidates. Look at checks and exchanges first before moving onto other possibilities. After you have done so, start calculating! Move to the second move candidate as soon as you have evaluated the first one. This is a technique described in the A. Kotov book "Think Like a Grandmaster". Of course, there are exceptions to the techniques described in the book, because some positions are more complex than others, there is also a time component present, but generally, it will give you a great basis on how to improve your calculations. My suggestion would be to take a piece of paper, set a middlegame position, and start calculating. Write down all you see on this piece of paper. If you do it correctly, you should build a tree with each calculation that you make. Set a time limit for yourself and always do this exercise over the board. Don't do it on your computer, your phone, or directly from a book. The dimension of the board is different, and this plays a very important role once you play in an OTB tournament.

Solving Puzzles

Solving puzzles is very closely connected with calculating skills improvement. I will divide the puzzles into "easy real game puzzles", "difficult real game puzzles", and "studies".

Easy Real Game Puzzles

These puzzles generally have a forced character and are solved within 0-5 moves. Once you play a chess game in a tournament, you will notice the true value of solving such puzzles. They will prepare you for spotting chess geometry and typical attacking motifs without breaking a sweat. They will also put you in a competitive state of mind, where you will search for each position as if there was a forced mate.

Difficult Real Game Puzzles

These are good for improving your calculation technique, since they often involve tactical and positional motifs. Best to do them over the board. This is the closest you will come to the real game situations.

Studies

Many chess players don't like solving studies. Studies are seldomly logical and are usually very different to what chess players are accustomed to. However, they are always very aesthetic and demand full use of one's imagination! This is exactly why you shouldn't neglect them. Take some time to solve them in order to improve your imagination.

Bear in mind that as over the board tournament approaches, you should be solving your puzzles almost exclusively over the board and not from the computer or a piece of paper. The dimension of a 3D chess board is significantly different. It takes time to adjust your perception to this exact dimension.

Analyzing The Classics

In the modern age of online chess programs, it's easy to forget about the fundamentals of chess. However, it is vital for our overall understanding and skill to study the classic chess games played by world champions. It is best to study these games on the chessboard and not while you are waiting in line or at the post office. Try to find books with written comments and analysis by the authors themselves. Pay special attention to their thought process and try to understand every move that has been made.

Playing

Most importantly, you must play chess – not merely prepare to play it. Whether it is over the board or on an internet chess platform, try to find strong opposition when playing training games. The stronger they are, the better types of questions they will be asking! Try to play Grandmasters if possible and try to communicate with them after the games. Ask them what they think, where you made mistakes, or where you could improve.

Don't play hundreds of games at a time. You will get tired in the process. You will also start to play worse and get frustrated. Be disciplined and play for a limited time. Take a look at your games afterward and ask yourself how good your openings were. Also, assess how you treated the middlegame and consider if there was a theoretical endgame that you didn't play well. Always try to come up with specific conclusions.

Staying Fit!

If you think a game of chess has nothing to do with your physical condition, you would be absolutely wrong. In order to keep your concentration through a 4-hour game, you need to be physically and mentally fit. Imagine the few hours of preparation you'll require before a game. It is followed by a game which lasts from 3-5 hours, which will then continue for a week – or more! If you're out of shape, you will get tired, lose your focus, and end up blundering and losing your games due to time troubles. Plan your workouts accordingly as well. It will serve you well in the B tournament as well.

Conclusion

Chess isn't a sport like several others, and its battles are classic. There is continually a subordinate and a war of excellent and evil. It is a game with a first-rate approach and problematic traps and attacks. The chess set focuses on the concept that the king is the most treasured chess piece on the chessboard. If each player declares the check, the priority is to defend the king at any cost. If you can't save the manipulate king, the game is over, and you lost a verification officer.

As a whole lot as chess is a method of recreation, your attitude is excellent. He is almost continually a player who performs a chess recreation if his mentality is dangerous. There is a connection between seriousness and focus, so the greater serious you are, the greater the targeted you're.

Another awesome manner to enhance your chess is to play quite a few games. The more you play chess and the extra experience, the greater you may learn and grow to be familiar with the sport. The extra you play, the more you will begin to investigate your moves and techniques at a whole new level, as your brain reminiscence has improved.

Utilizing chess machine guidelines can help you in improving your sport and provide your adversary in a favored position. Not anything works; practice every open door you have, and you'll see a huge improvement in your recreation.

At final, you at long closing figured out the way to play chess. What's more, presently, you are sufficiently able to assign or even win against numerous players.

Bonus Chapter: Tips for Beginners

The game chess is definitely an addicting game and a lot of people get fascinated by it. A person requires both skill and strategy in order to succeed in playing this board game. After knowing the components of the game, the basic rules, and other important information about chess, what you need to do is practice in order to improve your chess skills. It does not necessarily require one to be a genius in order to start playing chess. Here are some friendly tips and suggestions for beginners of chess:

1. During your first few matches, you can record the moves you have made. In this way, you can analyze your strengths and weaknesses in every game and see if the same patterns occur in your games. Find out the moves you think were done wrong so that the next time you can improve your game and do better.

2. In order to know more strategies and improve your skills in playing, you can study the games of different grandmasters. A lot of this information can easily be found online. You can watch videos and tutorials so that you can gain more insight about the game.

3. Do not consider some pieces inferior as compared to the others. It is important to remember that each piece has its own value to your game. Do not directly consider your Pawns as the useless. If used properly, they can be very helpful in stepping up your gameplay.

4. Also, don't forget to use all the pieces on your board. Do not just keep moving one or two pieces around because it can give you a lot of checks. You need to utilize your whole army and maximize all possible means of winning the game. One mistake that beginners usually commit is the use of only a few of the pieces in the game. Keep your board alive by moving all your pieces during the game.

5. The Queen is the most important and versatile piece you have. Try to protect it as much as possible but if you ever lose it do not also think that the game is over and you have no more chance of winning. Some people being to play carelessly once they lose their Queen. This is a wrong notion because other pieces are still present and besides, you still have pawns that can possibly be promoted to a new Queen.

6. Before making any movements on the board, think about it twice and do not act on impulse. For beginners, your games are not usually under time pressure so you have the luxury to think about your moves properly in order to avoid mistakes. Analyze the best possible responses you can do with regards

to your opponent's move. Also, think about the possible moves your opponent might do to counter your own moves. Constantly keep track of the moves done by both sides so that you can avoid making mistakes.

7. Always be alert and maintain focus while playing. During the game, a lot of distractions may be present around. Try to maintain your attention on the game so that you can keep track of the movements on the board. Some people tend to relax and lose focus which is why they are prone to miss out on the moves done by their opponent. If you keep looking away, you might not notice that your opponent is already building a strategy in order to trap your king.

8. Practice makes perfect. In almost anything you do, whether it is a sport or a hobby, you need to continuously practice in order to improve your skills from time to time. The same thing applies to chess. For beginners, it is advisable to practice regularly and have a partner to play along and learn with. Patience is a virtue that is why do not get disappointed if during your first few matches you still find it hard to win. After some time, you will find it easy to read your opponent and create your own game strategies as well.

Made in the USA
Las Vegas, NV
10 December 2022

61723721R00103